CABINET PUDDING

CABINET PUDDING

ANDREW NICKOLDS

Methuen

METHUEN

1 3 5 7 9 10 8 6 4 2

First published in Great Britain in 2002 by
Methuen Publishing Limited
215 Vauxhall Bridge Road
London SW1V 1EJ

Copyright © 2002 Andrew Nickolds

Andrew Nickolds has asserted his rights under the Copyright, Designs and
Patents Act, 1988, to be identified as the author of this work.

Methuen Publishing Limited Reg. No. 3543167

A CIP catalogue record for this book is available from the British Library

ISBN 0 413 77285 3

Typesetting and design by Geoff Green @ Geoff Green Book Design
Printed and bound in Great Britain by
Creative Print and Design (Wales), Ebbw Vale

Contents

Introduction

"**H**ave you decided yet?"

"I think I'll start with the Aubergine Confit with Sauteed Morelle, Trompette and Girolle Mushrooms…"

That wasn't what Gordon Brown meant, and Tony Blair knew it. Once again the two men who were generally agreed to be the most powerful in the country (this was the summer of 2001, before television bosses had given Ant and Dec the seminal Saturday evening ITV slot) were sitting in a corner of Granita restaurant in London's Islington.

They rendezvous-ed in the same place, at the same time every year, like nostalgic lovers. But much had changed since that momentous first meal in 1994, when the romantic adventure began and the leadership of the party was settled over a handshake and two signatures, scrawled on a snowy napkin in New Labour's equivalent of blood - the raspberry coulis left over from Brown's lamb chop.

Granita had changed, that was for sure. No longer did stars of EastEnders sit in the window, angrily demanding privacy. There was now no sign of influential newspaper columnists like Allison Pearson, who in 1994 had come over to their table, introduced herself to the impressionable Blair and made various suggestions, later enshrined in the election manifesto as commitments to a minimum wage and an ethical foreign policy. Pearson and her fellow zeitgeist-meisters had long ago moved on to Pastures New, the salad bar down the road in London's Clerkenwell. Granita was now distinctly Old New Labour.

Suddenly it was the twenty-first century, and everybody seemed to be getting on - everybody except me, thought Brown, sinking deeper into his metal seat. At such moments his face and crumpled demeanour took on the look of the snooker player Jimmy 'The Whirlwind' White, sitting on the sidelines at The Crucible as he watched an opponent relegating him to runner-up yet again in the World Championships.

"A euro for your thoughts" said Blair lightly. That was another thing – the Prime Minister's ease with a joke. There had been a time when Brown could pretty well hold his own on the humour front, with the help of top TV scriptwriter John O'Farrell who was always on hand to text-message a couple of crackers through to the Chancellor at a Mansion House dinner or economic summit. "G8? Sounds like a sports car!" was one he fondly remembered, topping it with "Brazil - isn't that where the nuts come from?" But that was before O'Farrell had become a best-selling novelist, spoken of in the same breath as Tony Parsons and Alan Titchmarsh, and now Brown's pleas for quips went unanswered.

He did his best. "Giz the top job" said Brown, trying to sound flippant. But such crude directness only made Blair flinch, and he started looking hard at his menu. Oh no, thought Brown, I've done it again. Here comes another initiative.

His mind went back to the Granita meal a couple of years ago, the last time Brown had mentioned the possibility of moving his few sticks of furniture and shaving kit from Number 11 to Number 10 Downing Street. Blair's way of dealing with the question then had been to stare fixedly out of the window at Islington's busy Upper Street. At that very moment a mugger in a hooded Gap sweatshirt was relieving an innocent passer-by of her wallet, her house-keys, the keys to the gite in Normandy and her 4x4, and the milking stool from the city farm.

Nobody in the street saw the incident, as they were all studying their mobile phones. Outraged, Blair leapt to his feet, rushed outside, hailed a cab and within half an hour was in the BBC's Newsnight studio in London's White City. There he announced wide-ranging plans to march muggers and louts up to cashpoints and impose instant £100 fines on them for their misdemeanours, after first (in the case of asylum seekers) providing them with bank accounts and £100 starter loans. Brown was left to pick up the bill, and the rest of the Cabinet to pick up the pieces from the fiasco.

Blair now put down his menu and fixed Brown with that familiar enthusiastic look of a newly-born hedgehog. "Y'know Gordon" he said ominously, "This time next year it'll be Her Majesty the Queen's Golden Jubilee. We should do something. Something big".

Brown started to gnaw at his fingernails, an ugly habit banned at home by his attractive new wife and PR czarina Sarah Macaulay. "Big like the Dome?"

"Forget the Dome. Everybody else has. To those people who said the Dome would be my epitaph, I say look at the figures in last week's General Election".

You mean the record low percentage turnout? thought Brown, but knew better than to say it. Not to be outdone in the ugly habits department, the Prime Minister stuck a corner of the menu into his ear and started cleaning it. "What about a cake?"

"A cake?"

"Not just a cake - the mother and father of all cakes. Something to go in the first paragraph of my *next* election manifesto".

So there it was. Brown had his answer. "But..." he started feebly.

"That's settled then". Blair got to his feet and headed

for the toilets. "Just off to shake hands with the unemployed" he joked, but then he turned back, his face serious. "Of which I might point out there are now one million less than when we first took office in 1997".

He was gone, and Gordon Brown found himself staring at Granita's brick wall.

CHAPTER ONE

The Events leading up to the Events of September 11

From The Berkhamsted Gazette,
29th August 2001

Local Schoolgirl Found Cabinet Papers On Canal Towpath

A local schoolgirl has found Cabinet Papers on a canal towpath. 17-year old Kerry Te Kanawa (no relation) was walking her dog Pete along the Grand Union Canal on Monday afternoon when they came across the vital government documents lying around an overflowing litter-bin.

"At first I thought it was kebab wrappers dumped by narrow-boaters up from Hemel", said Kerry, 16. "That lot are always using our stretch of the canal as their rubbish tip. Condoms, all sorts. But then I saw the papers had got writing and that on them and a royal thingy at the top. I'm like – duh!"

Big Brother

A Government spokesman described the top-secret minutes as "not at all important" and said the Prime Minister was "relaxed" about Kerry and Pete's discovery, though he refused to confirm or deny whether or not Mr Blair was incandescent with rage about the find.

"Anyway it was all really boring as far as I could tell", added Kerry who hopes to go to university after receiving good grades in her A-level results. "Just a lot of people going blah-di-blah-di-blah – like in the Big Brother house, only I'd never heard of any of this lot. Helen's my favourite, I hope she and Paul make a go of it".

Editorial from **The Daily Telegraph**,
30th August 2001

The Humiliation of Tony Blair

At last the control-freak seems to have got his long-over-due comeuppance.

Not at the hands of President Bush or General Pinochet or any of the other genuine world leaders to whom Blair regularly goes cap-in-hand.

No. The worst day for Blair since he was returned to power with his allegedly huge majority comes by courtesy of a humble Berkhamsted schoolgirl who was out and about enjoying the summer sunshine. She was not selling crack cocaine behind the bike sheds as the new Home Secretary would have us believe but innocently walking her dog, when she discovered Cabinet papers casually left lying around for all, our enemies included, to read.

It's young Kerry Te Kanawa we have to thank for a unique insight into the grubby workings of modern government. Some of these Cabinet discussions are reproduced opposite. We make no apology for that. The public has a right to know what is being done in its name.

The transcripts do not make happy or edifying reading. A proper administration would be spending its time and taxpayers' money responsibly, formulating an agenda for the anniversary of Princess Diana's death tomorrow.

Instead, what do we find? The Prime Minister riding roughshod over cowering Cabinet members as he concocts a ridiculous plan for a cake. What sort of cake or why we do not know, and the government refuses to tell us. Kerry's dog Pete behaved as dogs have since time immemorial – though how long it is before that becomes a criminal offence is anybody's guess – and innocently ate the first page.

At least when Margaret Thatcher was Prime Minister she had compelling reasons such as the Falklands War for riding roughshod, and the Cabinet over which she exerted her authority were the Nigel Lawsons, the Geoffrey Howes and the Ken Clarkes – genuine big beasts, unlike the present confederacy of dunces and pygmies.

The Blairs are currently sunning themselves in foreign climes at the expense of honest working people in the South of France. The Daily Telegraph would like to know why and how much. Not until we get answers to these questions can the ever-increasing gap between rich and poor sleep easy in its bed.

THE PRIME MINISTER (contd): ... And if we're really serious about this, if we truly want it to be a proper private-public partnership – a People's Cake – I'd look no further than Delia Smith.

THE DEPUTY PRIME MINISTER (RT. HON JOHN PRESCOTT): If you say so.

THE PRIME MINISTER: I just did. So, thoughts please. You've got three minutes.

PRESCOTT: Prime Minister, I wish when you said 'private-public partnership' you'd put the word 'public' first. Just for me?

THE PRIME MINISTER: Fair enough. Two minutes.

SECRETARY OF STATE FOR HEALTH (RT. HON ALAN MILBURN): Is Delia Smith one of us?

MINISTER FOR SPORT (RT.HON RICHARD CABORN): Isn't she something to do with the Fulham football team?

SECRETARY OF STATE FOR FOREIGN AND COMMONWEALTH AFFAIRS (RT.HON JACK STRAW): No that's Mohammed Fayed – I need to have a word with you about him, David.

SECRETARY OF STATE FOR THE HOME DEPARTMENT (RT. HON DAVID BLUNKETT): What? Who's that?

CABORN: Or did she play for them? I'm sure there's a Fulham connection.

PRESIDENT OF THE COUNCIL & LEADER OF THE HOUSE OF COMMONS (RT. HON ROBIN COOK): That's Gordon Ramsay you're thinking of. Gaynor swears by him.

PARLIAMENTARY SECRETARY TO THE TREASURY & CHIEF WHIP (RT. HON HILARY ARMSTRONG): Can't she think up any recipes herself, then? Proper little Second-Hand Rose isn't she...

MINISTER FOR WORK (RT. HON NICK BROWN): Ooh, back in the knife box, you!

MINISTER WITHOUT PORTFOLIO AND PARTY CHAIR (RT.HON CHARLES CLARKE): Girls, girls.

THE PRIME MINISTER: Look, can we agree on this please? Delia Smith, yes or yes?

MILBURN: Yes. Safe pair of hands.

BLUNKETT: Yes – bit of a looker too, from what they tell me.

NICK BROWN: Yes – safe pair of oven-gloves!

PRESCOTT: Who let him in?

SECRETARY OF STATE FOR TRANSPORT (RT. HON STEPHEN BYERS): Yes – but don't quote me.

THE PRIME MINISTER: Your secret's safe with us, Steve.

BYERS: I mean it.

SECRETARY OF STATE FOR INTERNATIONAL DEVELOP-MENT (RT. HON CLARE SHORT): Before we all get carried away by this...

STRAW: Here we go.

SHORT: I'd just like to say that I'm not happy.

STRAW: When is she.

SHORT: I mean, where are we going to make this big cake? I don't want to go back to my constituents in Ladywood and tell them it's another Home Counties carve-up...

CABORN: Hear, hear – so I suggest Wembley. It's only used two weeks every year for the tennis.

BLUNKETT: What about the Dome? [WHIMPERING FROM UNDERNEATH CABINET TABLE] What is it, Lucy love?

PRESCOTT: I meant to kick you, not the dog. You mentioned the 'D' word.

THE PRIME MINISTER: I appreciate your concerns Clare, I really do. And I've been listening to my constituents too. And what they tell me is this: "Hey Prime Minister, wouldn't it be, y'know, great if we could do something for all the people who've suffered a catastrophic loss of business during the foot-and-mouth epidemic?" And my answer, of course, is...

THE CHANCELLOR OF THE EXCHEQUER (RT. HON GORDON BROWN): "Yes, just as soon as the following five criteria are met. One..."

THE PRIME MINISTER: Sorry Gordon, time's up. Next business...

SECRETARY OF STATE FOR ENVIRONMENT, FOOD & RURAL AFFAIRS (RT. HON MARGARET BECKETT): Before we move on – what exactly is foot-and-mouth?

Date: 31/08/01
From: Jo Moore, Special Adviser
To: Everyone in the department – and anybody else
who knows me!

Hi,
In case we haven't met, Moore's the name…'and
Moore's the pity', as someone used to say at my
school! That young lady ended up working in a chemical factory, and the last I heard she'd lost both
her hands after a spillage. So I guess she won't be
tapping her keyboard and going on-line in a hurry!
    Anyway, this is to introduce yours truly and
wonder if anyone has any thoughts about what type
of Smiley Face font I should use at the end of this
and subsequent missives. I want informality to be
the keynote in this department as of now, so any
suggestions you have about this or anything else,
remember my door – and mail-box! – is always open.
    Jo

    PS Steve the big boss-man has asked me to attach
this report from the Cabinet office about documents
of ginormous importance being left in public
places. So be very very careful, as I say to my
kids when they're wearing their outside shoes in
the house. And if anyone can find out anything
about that little madam who gave those papers to
the press, well I didn't tell you this but there
might be one or two brownie points in it!

REPORT TO THE CABINET OFFICE

cc: HOUSE OF COMMONS LIBRARY
(to ensure maximum secrecy one copy will be lodged in the Library, and none in any of the places listed below)

In reply to the Cabinet Secretary's request of 1st September, the breakdown of the incidence and where-abouts of Cabinet and other highly confidential government documents left lying around during the period of the last 25 years is as follows:

37% Canal & River Towpaths
24% Trains or station platforms*
12% Backs of Taxis
11% Mayfair flats**
8% Wine bars & pubs
5% Hospitality room at 'Have I Got News For You' studio
2% Telephone kiosks (1% used for jotting down girls' business numbers, 1% used for mopping up juice from crumpled Ribena cartons)
1% Elsewhere (includes box on the back of pizza delivery bike, Clapham Common, Hampstead Heath, Swadlincote Miners' Welfare Club***)

*   Excludes Thatcher years 1979–90 when nobody associated with government travelled by train

**   Exclusively during Major years 1990–97. See Appendix breaking figures down into categories of: undisclosed third homes/honey-traps for Arab customers/Jeffrey Archer & Edwina Currie love-nests etc

*** Suspect (New Labour Minister) abandoned papers in haste after realising it wasn't a karaoke bar

Figures may need to be updated in coming months to allow for the rapidly spreading phenomenon of Spearmint Rhinos lap-dancing club

Conclusion: As more than 60% of these incidents occurred on the transport system, suggest passing figures on to that department for comment and preventive action

'Byers to deal'

September 2, 2001 (the day before war broke out - see later!)

Thanks for another superb and relaxing holiday. Food and facilities excellent as ever - a cut above the boiled sweet we were given to share between us on the Ryanair flight to Carcassone, I can tell you! This year we discovered a wonderful new route down into the village, a sunken track where the trees meet overhead, which means you're completely hidden from lurking cameras and Rory Bremner, who persists in turning up in his shorts expecting a game of celebrity tennis. Talk about biting the hand that feeds you.

But let's not spoil these last moments. I've been looking back at my and Cherie's previous entries in this book (we'll draw a veil over Kathryn's enthusiastic stab at drawing the Spice Girls back in 1998, though I'm glad to see it's still there, and for sale for £3000/4500 Euros). And I must say I find it hard to add anything original - the superlatives have all been used up. So if I may I'll just jot down a few personal thoughts, safe in the knowledge that my very good friend Alastair Campbell won't be able to get his hands on it and turn it into one of those Daily Mirror articles that go out under my name - so indigestible even chips wouldn't be seen dead in it.

As I sit here at the edge of the pool, a glass of something politically incorrect at my side, there's one immediate tip that comes to mind that I can pass on to future visitors. Don't be Prime Minister. It's getting so I can't do anything in the country's interests without its being completely misconstrued and twisted into an attack on New Labour. You'd think a simple gesture like planning an anniversary cake for Her Majesty's Jubilee would be warmly received, wouldn't you, especially in the Tory press. But suddenly I'm being treated like Marie Antoinette, with cake expenditure somehow being set against the number of old ladies left rotting on trolleys in hospital corridors.

Incidentally (and here's something to do on a rainy day) if you look at some of the old Visitors' Books in the library, you'll find that Marie Antoinette herself stayed here in the 18th century when she was Queen of France and she and Louis XVI were trying for a dauphin. Let's hope they found the atmosphere in the chateau just as conducive as we do! Marie was one tough lady and gutsed out her unpopularity, just like a certain predecessor of mine (I know I'm not supposed to say that, but what the hell, I'm on holiday).

So, sorry guys, all this sort of thing does is make me even more determined. When I get back tomorrow it's going to be a case of No More Mister Nice PM. This cake project will be something enjoyed by everybody and will stand as...

Oh rats – there's Leo and it's my turn. Thanks again to all the staff at the chateau and sorry about Euan and the wine-cellar. What he earns in his gap year should just about cover it. A bientot, hopefully...   Tony (Blair)

CHAPTER TWO

Re-enter The
Prince Of Darkness

PETER MANDELSON sat looking at the telephone. Out of deference to his constituents in working-class Hartlepool, it was an old black bakelite affair, with a dial instead of push-buttons, and a flex twisted into several impenetrable knots. Just like my tummy thought Mandelson, as the phone refused to surrender under the pressure of his basilisk stare and ring.

On the floor around the black leather and chromium Parker Knoll – the room's one item of furniture – lay scattered the day's newspapers. They were full of the latest exploits of Tony Blair's new best friend Lord Birt, recently appointed as the Prime Minister's Strategy Adviser. The former Chairman of the BBC had been anxious to make his mark and had proposed an idea for solving the ever-burgeoning crisis on the roads. It had come to him while looking out of his window at Television Centre towards London's busy Westway flyover.

Put simply, it was to encourage every motorist in the country to travel by hot-air balloon. This would be environmentally friendly and, crucially, would free up the motorways for aircraft to taxi along until they spotted a bit of empty air space. The opinion of the celebrated balloonist and ex-litter supremo Sir Richard Branson had been sought; he pronounced the plan 'brilliantly sound'.

But the papers were full of derision for this example of 'Blue Sky Thinking', and Mandelson couldn't but feel a pang of jealousy. That derision should have been directed at *him*. It seemed like only yesterday that Mandelson himself had occupied the role of Strategy Adviser, and he still had several thousand laminated business cards to prove it, with discount ticket offers for the Millennium Dome on the back.

Not that the saturnine grandson of Ernest Bevin, – 'Bobby' to New Labour intimates – bore his old friend 'Birty' any ill will. The two of them went way back, to the heady days of London Weekend Television in the early 80s when they were fresh-faced researchers on the award-winning *Clive James Takes the Piss Out of Everybody Less Intellectual.* And after the notorious 'outing' incident on Newsnight by the frankly unfanciable Matthew Parris, the Chairman had come to his old colleague's rescue, decreeing in a memo that every 'Peter Mandelson is gay' comment had to be prefaced with 'We're not allowed to mention that...'

Anyway, thought Mandelson (picking up the phone to check for the umpteenth time, only to hear the dialling tone yet again) grudge-bearing was in no way part of his make-up. Though you might not think that if you listened to the petulant tones of his so-called better half Reinaldo, who even now was probably blabbing about their snit over the breakfast table to anyone who'd listen in the charity shops of Hartlepool's garment district.

Their recent summer holiday had not been a success, and had ended with an embarrassing scene in front of fellow-guests on board Geoffrey Robinson's luxury long-boat The Herald of Free Enterprise – the name had come available after the 1987 Zeebrugge disaster and Robinson, never one to miss an opportunity, had snapped it up. Robinson's enemies alleged that he kept the boat on the move and listed it as his main residence in England as a way of avoiding council tax, but that was to belittle his generosity, as small-minded people with no money were typically prone to do.

What had really irked Mandelson's partner was not

the official reason given for the row in his letter of apology to their host – that it was about whose go it was to roll up their check-shirted sleeves and tackle the next lock in the flight on the Grand Union Canal. It was the fact that instead of admiring his friend's dexterity with the lock handle, Mandelson had chosen that moment to read some Cabinet papers instead.

Though not technically part of the Government after resigning for the second time in three years, Mandelson was still on Downing Street's mailing list, and he liked to keep an eye on what was going on, who was in, who was out, and who was sleeping next to whom in Cabinet meetings. He'd even contrived to hang on to a ministerial red box, with the cheeky initials 'PM' embossed in gold.

Mandelson was especially intrigued by Tony Blair's idea about a big cake, and was starting to turn his mind to how this feelgood project could best help the New Labour experiment. But then the papers were rudely snatched out his hand and hurled onto the canal bank with an oath by his fuming significant other. They'd barely spoken a word since, not even during the ten-hour delay at Watford Junction waiting for a driver to be trained and sent from Euston.

And now Blair was in Hartlepool for the day and there was no communication from him either. The Prime Minister was due to cut the ribbon and open a new Lottery-funded learning centre (or 'Learning Centre, Learning Centre, Learning Centre' as it said on the official plaque). Time was Mandelson would have been at his side, reminding Blair to perform the ceremony with his back to the crowd so as not to give the local press an easy 'More Government Cuts' photo-opportunity. But that was then. Now he wasn't needed, discarded like a handful of used Kleenex round a bed…

The black bakelite telephone rang. There was the familiar voice on the other end of the line. Mandelson's heart leapt. Blair got straight down to business.

"They want me to play something to christen the new music room".

"Have you brought the Fender Telecaster?"

"Of course, it's in the boot. What d'you reckon? Something by S Club 7 – that's Anji Hunter's idea – or Things Can Only Get Better, or Stairway to Heaven?"

Peter Mandelson savoured the moment, his eyes sparkling as the boyish frond of hair fell across his face. He was halfway up that stairway himself.

Bobby was back.

Date: 10/09/01
From: Dan Corry, Special Adviser
To: Jo Moore, Special Adviser (snap!)

Hi Jo,
Many moons ago you e-mailed the department wondering if we could dig anything up on this girl who just happened to find — big inverted commas! — the Cabinet papers on the towpath.

Well I called a mate who works for BBC South-East and asked him to check if they had any news footage of her — cost me a promise to throw my wicket away next time we play their team — but my hunch paid off cos low and behold there she is with her schoolchums getting her A-level results on the local news, screaming down her mobile "Oh-my-God-I've-got-an-A-in-Modern-Studies!!". And then doing the same thing for the cameras again as she wasn't hysterical enough on the first take.

Now this would you believe is the same girl who said she'd never heard of anybody mentioned in the Cabinet papers! Course it could just mean she got a crap education or the results were buggered up by Edexcel as usual, but I dug a bit deeper and found out that her Mum who goes by the name of Joyce is a leading member of the Women's Institute — and we all know what the WI think of New Labour! This Joyce also goes to regular meetings of something called the Hemel Hempstead Quilters, which could be a Tory far-right front.

It all smells a bit, n'est-ce pas? Shall I keep investigating?
Cheers, Dan
PS Like the smiley face idea. ☺ I sometimes

personalise my e's by going into Printer Options and messaging in different colours. Try it!

From: Jo Moore
To: Dan Corry

Hi Dan,
This is good work, keep it up. Will try out your colour idea. Like the Hogwarts Wizard lettering?
Jo ☺

From: Martin Sixsmith, Director of Communications, Department of Transport [DOCDOT]

To: Dan Corry
cc: Jo Moore
Dear Dan and Jo,
A little bird (actually a highly-placed former BBC colleague) tells me that the BBC news archive is being used for matters of a possible political nature. If you're thinking of doing this sort of thing would you please run it by me first, as I'm the one who's accountable to the Minister (my job description is attached).
Thank you. Martin (this message timed 17.23 and thirty seconds).

From: Jo Moore
To: DOCDOT
Sure, if you want to make a federal case of it.
Jo ☹
Message timed…oops sorry, dropped my watch. Will let you have it tomorrow, in triplicate.

From The Desk Of The Delia Smith Corporation

Today's Delia Thought:

'Everybody is famous for fifteen minutes, but a celebrity chef is famous for fifteen minutes at Gas Mark Five/220'C!'

10th September 2001

Dear Tony,

I've had someone check my diary, and I'm terribly sorry to say it looks like ('looks as if'?? **Memo** – suggest 'Delia's Book of Grammar') I'm just going to be rushed off my feet this autumn/winter/spring and therefore won't be able to give your excellent Jubilee Cake idea the attention it deserves.

For starters (as we say) I'll be launching the next BBC TV series, which I hope will be of some practical help to those just starting out on the food road. The format is 'How To Open A Tin Of...' and the programmes are as follows:

Episode 1 – Tuna
Episode 2 – Pineapple rings
Episode 3 – Pineapple Chunks
Episode 4 – Pink salmon
Episode 5 – Cling peaches
Episode 6 – Tomatoes
– and the Christmas Special – Ham...and what to do when the key breaks!

No rest for the wicked, because after that I'm needed to perform the State Opening of Parliament, before jetting off to the South Seas for a very flattering ceremony – apparently the powers-that-be down there have named an uninhabited atoll after me ('Delia'). I tried telling them that something pretty like 'Nigella' would be far more appropriate for an unkempt and craggy sea-girt lump, but they wouldn't take No ('Noh' in Hawaiian!) for an answer.

Then it's off with the grass skirt and on with the black frock to an Oxford English Dictionary do – seems the new edition uses 'Delia' as a noun – a proper one I trust! Just drinks and picky bits – haven't even got time to sort those out myself, so have suggested that one of the up-and-coming boys like Anthony Worrell Thompson might be glad of the work, now he's not on television quite as much as he thought he would be.

So you see Tony, I'm up to my neck. Also, I hear from the money men that my 'Delia' website has just lost around £60m so have to try and sort that out – one or two Norwich City players could be in for a bit of a shock. Of course if they care to read 'Delia Smith's Christmas' they'll find out how to give the kiddies a smashing time, despite having to cater on a severely restricted budget.

Sorry to have to disappoint you. Why not let Glenys Kinnock demonstrate her baking skills? If she's got time to belittle her betters she's surely got time to break a few eggs into a bowl (you'll need about 40,000 by my calculations).

Love,

Delia

Date: 11/09/01
From Jo Moore

To: Everybody
Just got back from lunch with Big Boss-Man Steve
(where are you all, by the way? It's like the place
has been evacuated. Is there some good sport on the
telly or something?)
Anyway B B-M S tells me Delia Smith has said no to
doing the Jubilee Cake. I know one set of videos
that's going straight in my bin when I get home!
Hope this glitch doesn't get out, this place has
more leaks than, I dunno, a leaky sieve! But here's
a thought in case it does and the brown stuff (and
I don't mean gravy!) hits the fan..
Today might be a very good day to bury bad news.
Councillors' Expenses?
Jo (And just for you, Martin – Message timed
14.55pm)
PS What do people think of my new colour scheme, a
different one per paragraph?

Jo ☺

To: Jo Moore
From: Dan Corry
Just got your e-mail. Bit terse and extreme I
thought. Do you really mean that? Oh, and did you
hear about Delia Smith? Should I run a Tory-
sympathiser check on her like I did on those other
women?
Dan

CABINET OFFICE
NEWS RELEASE

CAB 279/01

Following informal discussions between the Prime Minister and Iain Duncan Smith the newly-elected Leader of the Opposition, and in view of the Events of September 11, it has been agreed that things can and will never be the same.

Accordingly, Her Majesty's Government and Her Majesty's Opposition have decided that party posturing and tired cliches have no part to play in today's political climate. Life is too short. Under the 'pairing' system used in House of Commons voting, each side has therefore agreed to drop the following from its vocabulary with immediate effect:

The Government

18 years of sleaze
Level-playing field
Partnership
Empowerment
Joined-up
Drawing a line in the sand
Target/Challenge/Opportunity
Ring-fence
New money
Pro-active
Education x3
Nothing ruled in/out
Fat Cats
Third Way

Let us be absolutely clear

The Opposition

4 years of sleaze
Spin/Spin-doctor
Tony's Cronies (and any derivation, eg 'Silvio
Berluscroni')
Sound-bites
Cash-for-anything
Public ownership
Unelected
Gays/lesbians
Unelected gays/lesbians
Will he now come to the House and apologise
Two Jags
Infatuation with big business
So-called Third Way
Let us be absolutely clear

TRANSCRIPT OF BRIEFING GIVEN TO LOBBY JOURNALISTS

[Note: Briefing conducted under new guidelines as outlined in Cabinet News release CAB 279/01]

Government Spokesman: You'll appreciate that these are very tense times for the Prime Minister as he prepares to fly to Washington to meet President Bush, so if you could please confine your questions to the matters of most urgent importance to your readers?

Woman from Daily Mail: How does Tony Blair feel now he's been humiliated by Delia Smith?

Man from Daily Telegraph: Would you describe this as the worst moment for Tony Blair since he came to power...?

Woman from Daily Mirror: After Deliagate, has the government got 40,000 eggs on its face?

Man from Daily Telegraph: ...And if not, which was the worst moment? The fuel crisis? The Dome fiasco? Not being the alleged father of Liz Hurley's baby?

BBC Political Correspondent Andrew Marr: Does the Prime Minister perhaps feel a bit like someone who's walked in after a hard day at the office providing for his family, only to be hit over the head with a rolling pin by his irate wife in a pinny for coming home late?

Woman from Daily Mail: Did Blair burst into tears after the humiliating Delia snub or what?

Man from Daily Express: Would the Prime Minister consider acknowledging the importance to the country of our ethnic communities by letting the cake recipe be provided by a good-looking bit of Asian crumpet with her top off?

Government Spokesman: Well, let's be absol...erm...we're not ruling anything...hang on, erm...as far as Tony's con-

cerned it's time to draw a line in...shit...and be pro-
act...look, sorry, I've gotta shoot, I'm picking the kids up
from their bog-standard comprehensive, Christ can I still
say that?

Girl from ITN (shouting across road): Will the Prime
Minister be resigning?

CABINET OFFICE
NEWS RELEASE

CAB 280/01

The previous release from this Office [Cab 279/01] is no
longer operative, with immediate effect. This is not to say
that it has been ruled out. Or in.

Welcome to the Diary of
Kerry (The Vampire Slayer!)

Do Not Enter, on pain of having all your blood sucked out – gross! Actually whoever's reading this, right, can please Enter in case anything happens to me.

Because guess what – I'm being stalked! Whoa! I've been getting millions of these seriously weird text messages. And a guy coming up to me in Berkhamsted High Street with a clipboard and way uncool trousers out of Mackays front window, and he's like 'Would you describe yourself as 'Very Political…Quite Political…Not A Bit Political' I'm like 'I'd describe myself as Very Per-leeaase – just leave me alone will you Dude?!' But he doesn't take the hint, he comes lumbering like the Living Dead after me shouting "If you had been old enough to vote at the last Election (didn't know there was one) would you have voted for William Hague the baldy man? And if not how do you feel about Ian Duncan-Smith, the slightly less baldy man? Do you think he's Very Sexy…Quite Sexy…?" As if.

I only got rid of the creep by jumping on a bus and getting off in Hellmouth (my new name for Hemel Hempstead!) and that's when the text messages start: Would I vote for New Labour if it meant getting pizza or movie vouchers or free CDs? Why do I need any more of them, I've already got a pension scheme, right?

Now my Mum's being a real sadquake and pretending she's being stalked too! Yeah, right. Tell me about it. "I was just off to the Quilting last night" she says, and this guy comes up to her and asks if she's ever posed for a nude WI calendar! In your dreams, Ma – correction, nightmares, just thinking about it makes me want to puke. But, better hold my guts together, it's time for my driving lesson. I know that bitch goddess Hecate the instructress is just dying to fail me. Later, slayerettes!

The Friday People

Sarah Maternity-Leave,
Managing Director, Sow's Ear Publishing,
The Old Kebab House,
6, Windmill Street
London W1P 1HF

24 September 2001

Dear Sarah,

Getting the name change out of the way first – you may remember us as the Connell Jackson Knowles Literary Agency (founded 1906), but we did a bit of research and found that 'Friday' with its connotations of 'Yessss! It's nearly the weekend!' had the right kind of up-front enjoyment factor characterised by our authors and the books that we know YOU want to publish.

We really do cover the waterfront with our client list Sarah, and if you're in the market for coffee-table or airport or toilet non-books, look no further than us, The Friday People. F'rinstance, this week we're very very excited to have secured a deal for first-look at any manuscript produced by any children produced by Tony Parsons and Julie Burchill in the event that they get back together again. Not looking very likely right now, but you never say 'never' in publishing!

I'm very pleased indeed to be enclosing a sample chapter of the forthcoming memoirs of a real heavyweight, no less a personage than the Deputy Prime Minister John Prescott. Now this is not your average beach read and I know that usually polit-lit spells kiss of death. But Sarah, when you've read this explosive material I'm convinced that you won't want to let this slip through your hands, the way you did at Penguin when you thought nobody would want to read about a sad woman smoking and getting drunk all the time.

I'd be grateful if you could let me have an answer (hopefully 'Oui') by the end of tomorrow, as the sharks are circling the boat and they smell the blood of a Whitbread nominee! I'm looking at an advance of 250k.

See you in Frankfurt if not before,

Byeee,

Pepsi Knowles

A Man Called Prescott

May-June 2001 – That Punch and Its Aftermath

Under normal circumstances a Deputy Prime Minister resorting to pugilism in the street, instead of the cut and thrust of debate that is the norm in our democracy and thankfully has been so throughout recent history, would have instantly relegated me to the back benches with a flea in my ear to rival the cauliflower ear of that fellow in Rhyl who had been unwise enough to hurl an egg in my direction after a long and frankly tiring day on the hustings.

But Tony Blair didn't need any of his precious focus groups (hocus-focus if you ask me, not that anybody did) to tell him that this was just the kind of no-nonsense slugger he wanted by his side during the forthcoming bruising election campaign, a man who gave as good as he got and returned it with the kind of compound interest that wasn't determined by Eddie George but had been acquired in the souks of Zanzibar and merchant ships in the Far East. And when in June 2001 we were returned to power with an equally thumping majority, I was duly given my reward for continuing loyal service. As official government documents that went out under my name put it at the time:

'I head a new Office of the Deputy Prime Minister in the Cabinet Office. I am supported by a Minister of State, Barbara Roche, and by a Parliamentary Secretary, Christopher Leslie and by Lord Macdonald of Tradeston CBE and Baroness Morgan of Huyton for business in the House of Lords. As First Secretary of State I will continue to deputise for the Prime Minister as required, drawing on the resources of other parts of the Cabinet Office as necessary. I will oversee the work of the Social Exclusion

Unit, which reports to the Prime Minister through me. I am also responsible for the Regional Co-ordination Unit and the nine Government Offices of the Regions.

On international matters I will support the Prime Minister by seeing visiting dignitaries; undertaking overseas visits; and overseeing the work of the International Public Service Unit. I also carry Ministerial responsibility for the British Irish Council and will deputise as necessary for the Prime Minister at meetings of the Council. I will continue to play a role in international climate change discussions and negotiations on behalf of the Prime Minister. In addition, I will chair new Cabinet Committees on Domestic Affairs and on Nations and the Regions; and new sub-Committees on Social Exclusion, Regeneration and Energy Policy. I will continue to chair the Committee on the Environment."

Bit hi-falutin, not to say garbled – the mangling of the English language by civil servants was one aspect of prioritisation I was determined to take under my wing in addition to my many other onerous duties outlined above. In a nutshell you could boil it down to one inescapable fact: when Tony was away, I was in charge. In no way was I sidelined or demoted. Right?

To illustrate the blindingly obvious truth of this statement, when Tony was called to Washington for war consultations with President Bush after the tragic and in many ways momentous events surrounding the attack on the World Trade Center on September 11 2001, I was called into action to do a bit of fire-fighting of my own and chair an emergency Cabinet meeting to discuss arrangements for the Queen's Golden Jubilee the following year (2002):

TRANSCRIPT OF CABINET MEETING

THE DEPUTY PRIME MINISTER (RT. HON JOHN PRESCOTT): First up everybody – thanks for coming. Bit of a schlep, but I think it'll be worth it.

SECRETARY OF STATE FOR THE HOME DEPARTMENT (RT. HON DAVID BLUNKETT): You're sure he can't hear us?

PRESCOTT: Who, Peter Mandelson?

BLUNKETT: No – Tony.

PRESCOTT: He's in Washington, David. And Mandelson's miles away trying to find out where we all are, I wouldn't mind betting, ha ha.

BLUNKETT: Right. I've wanted to be able to say this since the turn of the century. Dome! Dome Dome Dome! Biggest White Elephant in history! Complete waste of public money! Dome Dome...why is my voice echoing?

SECRETARY OF STATE FOR FOREIGN AND COMMON-WEALTH AFFAIRS (RT.HON JACK STRAW): Because that's where we are – inside the Millennium Dome.

BLUNKETT: Really? What's it like?

SECRETARY OF STATE FOR TRANSPORT (RT. HON STEPHEN BYERS): Just like it always was – empty. I didn't say that.

BLUNKETT: Shouldn't you be in Washington too, Jack?

STRAW: Bit of a delay with my passport – something to do with having short hair on a student demo at Grosvenor Square back in the 60s.

PRESCOTT: I'm sure our loss is America's gain. Anyway, I expect you're wondering why I've asked you all here.

PRESIDENT OF THE COUNCIL & LEADER OF THE HOUSE OF COMMONS (RT. HON ROBIN COOK): Not quite all. I don't see the Chancellor sitting with us round this vertical perspex table from the Office Furniture of the Future Zone.

PRESCOTT: There's a good reason for that, Robin. Tony doesn't want Gordon to know about this discussion until the time and conditions are right.

COOK: To coin a phrase.

PRESCOTT: Yeah, right. Anyway, anybody got any views so far?

SECRETARY OF STATE FOR INTERNATIONAL DEVELOP-MENT (RT. HON CLARE SHORT): Well I have to say I'm not happy.

STRAW: We all know you have to say that, but you don't know what we're talking about yet.

SHORT: Is it the cake?

PRESCOTT: It is, as it happens. [GROANS] Now then, settle down. After the Delia Smith setback, Tony is very keen to get this project back on track.

BYERS: Is that some kind of snide reference to the railways?

PRESCOTT: Do what?

BYERS: Because I'd just like to point out that I am now the Secretary of State for Transport...

MINISTER FOR WORK (RT. HON NICK BROWN): And I will have vengeance!

BYERS: I beg your pardon?

BROWN: 'Gladiator' joke. Sorry.

BYERS: Apology noted.

PRESCOTT: Just relax Stephen, will you? Don't forget you're the new kid on the block. I did that bloody job for four years. My ambition used to be to make the trains run on time...then it was making the trains run...at the end I was happy just to make the trains!

[LAUGHTER & APPLAUSE]

I'm not normally one to blow my own trumpet, being in no way as adept as the late great Louis Armstrong in that department, but I have to admit I was quite pleased with that little bit of repartee. It certainly shut the boy Byers up, and after that it's fair to say I had Cabinet in the palm of my hand...

PRESCOTT: I still say you can't beat an old-fashioned jam sponge.

SECRETARY OF STATE FOR TRADE AND INDUSTRY (RT. HON PATRICIA HEWITT): Not very New Labour.

SECRETARY OF STATE FOR CULTURE, MEDIA AND SPORT (RT. HON TESSA JOWELL): Or Cool Britannia. We want to see young people sitting outdoors at pavement cafes, hailing waiters in a friendly socially democratic way to bring them a spritzer and another slice of...

PRESCOTT: We're not having any of that foreign carambiatta rubbish, girl. Not while I'm in charge.

SECRETARY OF STATE FOR HEALTH (RT. HON ALAN MILBURN): Jam sponge isn't exactly good for you though, is it.

COOK: Let's hear your thinking then, Alan.

PRESCOTT: I'm asking the questions. Let's hear your thinking then, Alan.

MILBURN: What about something with fruit in it? Tasty but wholesome?

JOWELL: And totally un-fun.

MILBURN: I don't know, we could get Lord Winston to dress up as a raisin to indicate its health-giving properties...

PRESCOTT: Lord Who?

MILBURN: Winston – Egregious Professor at Imperial College London.

STRAW: Yes, he'd say or do anything if it gets him on TV.

[BARRAGE OF COUGHING AROUND TABLE]

BLUNKETT: Before we decide what sort of cake it is, should-n't we discuss the means of production?

BROWN: Ooh – fiver in the swearbox, you!

BYERS: Er, If nobody minds me speaking as the new kid on the block – before we do any of this shouldn't we sell the idea to the British people?

PRESCOTT: Right – Tessa, could you get the Poet Laureate to knock something out? Time he sang for his supper, he's done bugger-all since the fuel crisis was called off.

JOWELL: It's done.

BLUNKETT: What did you have in mind, Steve?

PRESCOTT: Didn't you hear what I said, Beardie? Read my lips. Oh, sorry.

BYERS: Speaking as the new kid on the block, I suggest a public relations gimmick to ensure everyone's on-message and supports us in this venture.

BROWN: You had me on 'gimmick', Steve – remember Phoenix the Calf?

SECRETARY OF STATE FOR ENVIRONMENT, FOOD & RURAL AFFAIRS (RT. HON MARGARET BECKETT): Phoenix the what?

From The Berkhamsted Gazette,
26th September 2001

Leave Us Alone, Pleads Local Family

"You'd think they'd have something better to do after the events of September 11th" said Joyce Te Kanawa (no relation)(46) as she fought back the tears at her small terraced house in Shrublands Avenue which she shares with her pretty teenage daughter Kerry.

"What happened on September 11th, Mum?" jokes Kerry. A happy tight-knit single-parent family like any other, in other words. But for the last few weeks the Te Kanawas' life has been made a misery as they are pestered by phone-calls, text messages and strangers stopping them in the street soliciting their political opinions.

"It just used to be people asking you to sign things about people being tortured to death in Iran", said Joyce. "But this is much, much worse". She even claims to have been doorstepped Fleet Street style, as she visits her local quilting club (motto: Quilt While You're Ahead) in Hemel Hempstead.

Both Joyce and Kerry agree that the trouble started when a Gazette story about their dog Pete finding top-secret Cabinet documents on a canal bank was picked up and used by several national newspapers, without paying for it.

And Joyce has a message to whoever's behind the serial pestering. "I'd just like to say through the pages of the Gazette to whoever's behind this: No thank you very much, I do not want a New Labour cappuccino machine. And how I vote is entirely a matter between me and the woman who sits on the chair outside the polling station wearing the blue rosette".

"I wish Pete had eaten the lot now", says Kerry, who is still hoping to go to university.

CHAPTER THREE

The Long Road Back

"Here you go, Iain, get your speechifying gear round this".

Charlie Whelan, one half of the newly-formed Chaz 'n' Del Political Services Consultancy, gingerly lowered three pints of lager-top down onto the table and pushed one towards the newly-elected Leader of the Opposition. Across at the bar Derek 'Dolly' Draper, Whelan's 'partner in crime' as it said in jaunty letters on their company t-shirt, paid for three differently-coloured packets of Kettle Chips and brought them over.

"What's your preference, Iain?"

"Salsa please".

"Wise man. Top decision".

"Is it?"

"Yeah, cos it *is* a decision", said Draper, sitting down after first turning his chair round like a detective in an interview room. "Shows you to be a geezer what knows his own mind, and won't be pushed around by the likes of me saying that choosing the black Sea Salt packet might play better in the media. I think we've lucked into a good 'un here, wouldn't you say Chaz?"

"I would indeed Del" agreed Whelan. "Hold up - goal to us by the sound of it".

It was a Saturday afternoon during the party conference season and the three men were sitting in a pub within earshot of a leading London Premier League football ground. Their conversation was punctuated by roars from the faithful as the match ebbed and flowed. The sounds emanating from the ground suggested the crowd was currently getting good value for the £50 they'd paid at the turnstiles.

Iain Duncan Smith relaxed. He felt he'd successfully negotiated an important first hurdle. Unconsciously he cleared his throat.

"Nasty cough you got there, Iain", said Draper.

"Nasty but not necessarily unpromising" countered Whelan, as ever seeking to sniff out an angle. It was this always-look-on-the-bright-side quality that had helped him bounce back from his recent reverses. Being fired from Gordon Brown's team of special advisers for reasons of alleged treachery and back-stabbing would have been a stain on most people's CV. But within weeks Whelan had managed to parlay the reverse into a flourishing career on Radio 5 Live, a stall in Kensington Market selling House of Commons bric-a-brac, and a peak-time appearance on that night's 'Weakest Link Special – Disgraced Spin-Doctors'.

Draper, former adviser to Peter Mandelson, had arrived at his partnership with Whelan via a more circuitous route, after being fired for bragging about his Cabinet contacts during a function at the Westminster Banqueting Hall. Suspicions were aroused by the long queue of lobbyists winding its way into the lavatories to leave cash-for-influence in brown envelopes behind and on top of the cisterns. When portable loos or 'honey-wagons' started arriving in the Westminster car park to accommodate the overspill of bribes, the Government decided it had had enough, and Draper was told to clear his desk and be out of the loop by lunchtime.

But he like Whelan had turned the sacking to advantage. After getting into conversation with one of the honey-wagon drivers who had come on from Pinewood film studios, Draper decided to plough his redundancy money into the location catering business, and for a while his company 'Hello Dolly' thrived providing services to Lottery-funded 'Brit-pics'. Draper was even contemplating the prospect of an MBE in the not-too-distant future, which would have been a thoroughly-deserved smack in the kisser to his former employers.

The kids however became increasingly bored seeing East End gangsters hanging upside down and having their throats cut and testicles blown off to a jaunty 70s soundtrack – sometimes they shouted 'Fast Forward!' before the chainsaw had even been plugged in. Audiences dwindled, and Draper saw the way the wind was blowing when the likes of Jude Law and Vinnie Jones started arriving on the set with their own packed lunches. The last straw came the morning Ewan McGregor was obliged to break off from Obi-Wan Kenobi duties in the latest Star Wars blockbuster, to bring a pint of milk across to his thirsty mates filming 'You Are So Facking Dead 3'.

Luckily Draper was able to sell on the Hello Dolly franchise to the recently-fired Culture Secretary Chris Smith, before throwing his lot in with Whelan to form what the press was already calling 'this unholy alliance of spiv doctors'. But the chirpy survivors didn't care: "'We're back in beeswax" they chortled as they opened their new laptops and symbolically downloaded a consignment of fresh porn from the Internet.

It was this street-fighting feistiness that had led Iain Duncan Smith to share a pub table with what were on the face of it strange bedfellows. He produced a small tin from his waistcoat pocket.

"Anybody care for one of these?" asked IDS, clearing his throat again.

"What you got there, some 'e's?" asked Whelan, his eyes bright.

"Hey Chazza, that rhymes! You're a bleedin' poet my son"

"It's a Strepsil, actually". Duncan Smith was keen to get on.

"Put 'em away", said Whelan. "And keep the cough. Could be your USP during PMQs"

"Ooh narsty, what's that? Something women get?" Draper pulled a Kenneth Williams face.

"Prime Minister's Questions you wanker"

"*Wonker*, don't you mean?! Hagh hagh hagh". Draper laughed a Sid James laugh.

What about Prime Minister's Questions?" asked Duncan Smith, impatiently. The Tory conference was fast approaching, and he needed to make his mark. Also at £250 an hour for the Chaz n' Del consultation, the party coffers couldn't stand much more of this irrelevant backchat.

"Every time Tony Blair comes out with an answer, use your cough like a bullshit-detector, right? Like 'Oh yeah?' or 'Come off it pal' or 'I don't be*lieve* it', like Victor Meldrew. Guaranteed big woofers every time" said Whelan, wiping a bit of froth from the Leader of the Opposition's weekend tie.

"I don't know that I want big woofers" said Duncan Smith. "What I want is sound policies, not sound bites". He stopped. "Just a minute – that's quite neat, isn't it? 'Sound policies not sound b…'"

Draper sighed. "What are we going to do with this one, Chazzington?"

"What are *you* going to do, you mean" said Whelan, looking at the pub clock. "Got to get back to the match – I'm on in five minutes doing a half-time report for Five Live".

"Shouldn't you have been watching it?" said Duncan Smith, dismayed at the thought of cheated BBC listeners, already staggering under the weight of a crippling licence fee.

"Nah – take a shufti at the state of play then tell 'em what they want to hear. First rule of focus groups. Nice to make your acquaintance, Iain – the lavs are that way if you want to leave our fee in cash. Olive oil!"

"The cough ploy is all very well, and don't think I'm not grateful" said Duncan Smith after Whelan had gone, leaving a pile of business cards on the bar. "But I really must have something for the conference".

"Course you must. Course you must" said Draper. "In fact, you look like a geezer in serious need of a quilt".

"A quilt? Why a quilt?"

"Ah, wouldn't you like to know", said Draper. "Buy me another pint and let's see if we can't come up with something that makes Peter Lilley's conference sing-songs look really pathetic".

fat cat

Epicure Mammon at the Labour Party Conference in Brighton

Who's this putting on his top hat, polishing his patent leather shoes and making up for lost time? No, it can't be **Peter Mandelson** can it? Bad news, Brothers – it is! Ever since little Peter puffed out his chest and squeaked 'I'll Be Back' like Arnie in The Terminator, our new New Labour friends on the rubber chicken satay circuit have been quaking in their Gucci moccasins dreading a moment like this.

Mandy-About-Town has been seen getting his snout in a whole farmyard-full of troughs this week, from the **Enron** marquee via the giant battery-chicken conglomerate **HenCom** (rumoured to be engaged in a hostile takeover of **The Egg Marketing Board** – remember you read it here first!) then taking tea with **The Jam Today Consortium** and popping in to wish **Caster and Pollux Sugar Corp.** sweet dreams! Just as well those nice people from **Consignia** had been sent to Bournemouth by mistake, or Mandy's dance card would have been fuller than a **Connex** station platform at rush-hour!

But never let it be said our man forgets his roots, even if they are dyed!

He did find time to check out the **TUC** stand (that's not the savoury biscuits but the unsavoury unions!) It seems they were offering the prize of train tickets for two to Paris and a three-star hotel thrown in if anybody joined their ever-diminishing band. Seems a fair deal: France gets our trots, we get their asylum seekers! One for all and all for one – or rather none for them and thousands for us!

But strange to say Mandy didn't fancy Gay Paree, so it was off to Brighton beach for some TLC and mutual back-scratching in the **Arthur Andersen** tent. So what was behind this little **Cook's Tour**? Cream, jam and sugar – could it be a recipe for something…apart from another New Labour disaster?!

I'd put money on it – or maybe donate it to the party instead, and be *Sir* Epicure Mammon before you know it!

Editorial from **The Daily Mail**
9th October 2001

Disfigured TV 'comedian' plums new depths

Chris Morris has done it again. Remember Channel 4's so-called satirist who outraged ordinary decent folk and wasted the valuable time of personalities like Noel Edmonds and Carla Lane, by persuading them to condemn a non-existent drug called Cake?

Well now, in a breathtaking burst of originality, Morris has been bamboozling innocent schoolchildren and old age pensioners into thinking there's a new cake on the market called 'Drugs', and getting them to say on television how much they love it. Families have been reduced to nervous wrecks and forced to sell their houses, often at less than market value, after seeing their grannies nod and smile and tell a nationwide audience "I can't get enough of it. I'd live on drugs if I could, especially at Christmas and on my birthday".

Morris, who has an ugly mulberry birthmark on his face but typically conceals it with thick make-up, is a million times less honest than these hoodwinked innocents. But of course one would expect nothing less from Channel 4, the company that pays him a fat salary, most of which probably disappears straight up his nose.

But let's not lay the blame solely at Morris's well-heeled door. His clever little hoax, pathetic though it is, would surely never have left its diseased drawing-board had it not been for the government's obsession with the much-heralded, but still equally non-existent Jubilee Cake. Like the crackling of thorns under an empty pot, so is the laughter of a fool, a wiser man than Tony and Cherie Blair once said. Chris Morris and New Labour deserve each other. Both stink to high heaven.

BBC

Memo from Rod Liddle, Editor, Today Programme, to Controller Radio 4.

You asked for a transcript of the relevant section of today's Today programme, so here it is. I can only say in mitigation that at the time I was busy on the phone in the Control Room, planning this Saturday's live 'roadshow' from Bury when we'll be turning the whole programme over to the British National Party. I'll be attaching some of their specific proposals in a separate memo.

By the way, I have to say I think some of the BNP proηerit, especially dividing the network at 7.50 and putting out a separate 'Thought for the Day' for Muslims on Long Wave, and other ethnic minorities on Short Wave. After all, they do have a different calendar (don't they, or was that Pol Pot's lot?) and expecting them to listen to white middle-class vicars banging on about Christian religious holidays might cause unnecessary offence. Nice to see the BNP have such a positive attitude!

RL

TRANSCRIPT OF 'TODAY' PROGRAMME 10/10/01

JOHN HUMPHRYS: Joining us now to discuss that Chris Morris broadcast is the Home Office Minister Beverley Hughes.

BEVERLEY HUGHES: First of all let me say that I haven't heard the programme.

HUMPHRYS: Yes you have, we just played it to you.

HUGHES: You may have played it to me, but I wasn't listening. I didn't need to hear it to deplore it.

HUMPHRYS: Would you like to hear it again?

HUGHES: Let me tell you what I was thinking about instead.

HUMPHRYS: Briefly if you would, we've got a lot of e-mails about hedgehogs to get in before the Weather.

HUGHES: I was thinking about how our Prime Minister is currently engaged on matters of real international importance and not wasting his energy on...

HUMPHRYS: So he isn't interested in the people of this country and what they watch on television?

HUGHES: Of course he is, but I'm saying you're mistaken if you think that...

HUMPHRYS: Are you saying you've never made a mistake?

HUGHES: I'm sure I've made lots of mistakes.

HUMPHRYS: Would you mind naming some of them?

HUGHES: I didn't come on this programme to talk about my...

HUMPHRYS: The notorious Jubilee Cake, that's a bit of a mistake, isn't it?

HUGHES: I'm sure when you see the Cake you'll realise what a success...

HUMPHRYS: Ah yes, but that's the point, isn't it. We haven't seen it. Nor as I suspect a lot of people think, are we likely to, any more than we're likely to see a better transport system, or hospital waiting lists cut, or a referendum on the euro – it's all pie in the sky isn't it, if I can mix my culinary metaphors?

HUGHES: I didn't come on to talk about the euro...

HUMPHRYS: No, but now that we've got you, a lot of our listeners find it absolutely incredible that Jo Moore hasn't resigned over the infamous 'burying bad news' e-mail on September 11. What have you got to say to that?

HUGHES: If I can get back to the Chris Morris programme which I didn't see -

HUMPHRYS: Or are you just waiting for Mr Blair to phone

home so he can tell you what to do, like he's trying to tell the rest of the world? Not doing much running his own country, is he.

HUGHES: It's simply not true to say that the government has been out-sourced – day-to-day line-management is very much in place...

HUMPHRYS: I thought you'd been told to stop using language like that. Seems that was *my* mistake...

[DOOR SLAM]

HUMPHRYS: Has she gone? Yes, there she goes, typical woman. Oh well.

JAMES NAUGHTIE: Let me just tell you what's coming up after the news. We'll be looking at the rivalry between Tony Blair and Gordon Brown, which is the subject of a fascinating new book by James Naughtie who'll be here with John in the studio to discuss it.

HUMPHRYS: And talking of 'burying bad news', let me tell you about Bury which is where Saturday's programme comes from...

NAUGHTIE: Oh dear – that was worthy of Mark Lawson!

HUMPHRYS: Didn't take me all day to write it though, so watch it Jock.

NAUGHTIE: Who are you calling Jock, Taff?

CHAPTER FOUR

Remote Control

THE HOTEL SUITE WAS LIT only by the eerie glow from a TV screen as the pretty dark-haired woman edged in through the door, after first negotiating the rest of the hotel furniture that had been piled outside in the corridor.

"Thank you for seeing me, Godfather", she began.

Peter Mandelson, his lean features made even more cavernous by the light from the TV, shushed her. "Just a minute Jo. Listen and learn".

Jo Moore watched as Mandelson moved his lips in time with a recording of his celebrated " Where there is peace, let me bring discord" acceptance speech in Hartlepool in the small hours of Election Night, 2001. She smiled as he jabbed a triumphal finger in the direction of his defeated Socialist Labour Party candidate, a man wearing an Arthur Scargill costume.

Next year that same man had learned from his mistakes and campaigned in the 2002 local elections dressed as a monkey. He duly became the new mayor. But this was in the future. Mandelson for the time being seemed preoccupied with the past, and reliving the moment that he came back from the dead – literally, as several political commentators had hinted darkly. But it was the present that now preoccupied Jo Moore.

She kissed Mandelson's hand. 'Godfather, I come because I need your help'.

Mandelson froze the picture on a frame of himself

rising to speak in the House of Commons. He stroked Moore's hair as she knelt at his side.

"I have followed your career with interest, Jo. You have done well since I appointed you chief Press and Broadcasting Officer at the time of the 1997 election. But now I sense you are troubled at work".

"Yes, d'you know what somebody did?" said Moore, still seething over the latest office insult, "Defaced a cutting that said 'MOORE'S TRIUMPH' – it was about Demi Moore actually, but I didn't tell anyone that – stuck on the side of my computer, by turning the two 'O's into a pair of breasts".

Mandelson stared at her. "And what is the *real* reason that you come to see me about? Is it the notorious e-mail about burying bad news?"

There was no fooling this latter-day Machiavelli, thought Moore. His hair may be blacker, but otherwise he hasn't changed a bit. "Everybody says I should resign. What do you say, Godfather?"

"I say the road back from resignation to rehabilitiation is a long, hard and rocky one. A river runs through it. I know what it is to resign on a point of principle. But then I confounded my enemies by once more taking my seat at the Cabinet table on the right hand of the Prime Minister. But they conspired to make me resign again, didn't they. Oh yes. So I say – enough resignations already. Acts are best not committed in the heat of the moment, but should be allowed to cool – like revenge, a dish that is tastiest served cold".

"Hang on, let me get all this down", said Jo Moore, making a note with her famous anti-Militant Tendency ball-pen, shaped like the ice-pick that was used to assassinate Trotsky.

"Who do you suspect of drawing the breasts?" asked the Head of the Policy Network, after waiting until Moore had jotted down the words "Don't resign", underlined twice with a little flower above the 'i'.

"Some guy in the office. He doesn't like me being so close to Steve. Diddums wants to keep him all to himself"

"Steve as in Byers?" said Mandelson, suddenly revealing his side teeth. "My replacement at the Department of Trade and Industry?"

"Yes", said Moore, "Martin Sixsmith is sucking up to him big-time. I think it was him behind the leaked e-mail too. Has it got colder in here, or is it just me?"

"It's just you", said Mandelson. "As for the next step – I suggest you watch this and take heed".

He pressed the remote control with such vehemence that his thumbnail split the 'Play' button. But Moore was oblivious as she watched her mentor pronounce in the Commons on the events of September 11:

"My advice to America is – don't get mad, get even".

GEORGE ALAGIAH: ...Our Political Editor Andrew
Marr is at the Conservative Party Conference in
Blackpool – Andy, what's been happening up there?

ANDREW MARR: George, the Tories always look for a
bit of showbiz razzmatazz at these events, something to
give them a bit of a lift – and today they got it in
spades, delegates were saying they'd seen nothing like
it since the 1980s when Kenny Everett did the famous
duet with Freddie Mercury at Mrs Thatcher's Wembley
rally at the end of which they gave out free giant condoms, too late for them of course because they both
died of AIDS not long afterwards, Beelzebub's revenge
for 'Bohemian Rhapsody' you might say...

GEORGE ALAGIAH: Andy, what's been happening up
there?

ANDREW MARR: Well, you no doubt remember the
roasting Tony Blair got at the hands of the Women's
Institute last year when he ill-advisedly started talking
about changing little Leo's nappies in front of an audience who clearly were too old to have children,
though I suppose they may have seen 'Jerry Maguire'
or at least got it out on video, the Tom Cruise movie
with its famous catchphrase 'Show Me The Money',
well Iain Duncan Smith isn't quite Tom Cruise, not yet
at any rate unless you can count a cough as a catchphrase...

GEORGE ALAGIAH: Andy, what's been happening up
there?

ANDREW MARR: Well it was quite extraordinary, suddenly these middle-aged ladies from Hemel
Hempstead in Hertfordshire got up on stage and
unfurled to vast applause and a standing ovation last-
ing eight minutes – which was twice as long as Ann

Widdecombe's though of course Michael Howard didn't get one at all, how times change – a most enormous colourful quilt carrying the words 'Tony Tony Show Us The Cake', which was a kind of mixture of the catchphrase from Jerry Maguire and an old song called 'Dinah Dinah Show Us Your Leg' made famous if memory serves by a music-hall comedian called…

GEORGE ALAGIAH: Andrew Marr, thank you.

MEMO

For: TB's eyes only
From: Alastair Campbell
Date: 22/10/01
Subject: Everything going pear-shaped

Sorry I wasn't at the airport, but I've been chained to the desk. Anyway I'd have needed to hold up a piece of card with 'Prime Minister' on it in felt-tip, because quite frankly me and everybody else has forgotten what you look like.

While you've been out riding the range with Dubya in Marlborough Country planning to bomb the shit out of every enemy of the free world, things have been...well, I'll tell you how bad they are. Max Clifford's been on the phone offering to help out with an image makeover.

Everyone's saying everything's spinning out of control. Cobblers of course, but we've got to start delivering on even one election promise soon. I can try and keep the Jo Moore brouhaha going as long as I can, and I've asked Philip Gould to pull some opinions together on your new haircut, but that can only be a stop-gap measure.

What's more Gordon Brown's gone very quiet, a sure sign of trouble. I've been getting your kids to put on their 'Ibiza Anthems' CD at full blast, but not so much as a bang on the wall.

We need a bone to toss to the Great British Public and I suggest (I can't believe I'm saying this for Christ's sake) your cake. That little counter-jumper Shaun Woodward keeps scuttling round saying he's got a recipe for Madeira Cake (his in-laws used to govern Madeira apparently) that's been handed down for generations but he says he'll pretend to have got it off the back of a Stork margarine wrapper if we like. Tosser.

Whatever, somehow the cake's become a symbol for everything that New Labour isn't doing so I suggest we address this perceived paralysis and get our ass in gear, as the centurion said to Jesus on Palm Sunday.

Meantime all I can do is tell the rat-pack that you've come back to take personal charge of the whole situation. Yawn, but they still seem to buy it. Then the ball's in your court, buster. I'd write a gung-ho piece for the Daily Mirror but I gather your chips wouldn't be seen dead in it.

I'm in Italy watching football for a couple of days, mainly so I can sign this memo

                                                    AC, Milan.

MEMO

For: Tony
From: Anji
Date: 22/10/01
Subject: Cake Recipes

Been thinking about the conversation we just had. It's great
that you're taking personal control of the situation and
your ideas are as ever 150% brilliant (or 'awesome' as I've
heard kids on the train say). Just one or two nit-picks, then
I think we could be in an oven-ready situation.

1) Jane Asher. I know you're looking for a media-
friendly replacement for 'Dame' Delia (and goodness, wasn't
it clever of you to nip that honour in the bud!). I'm also
aware that she's the kind of name that means a lot to the
kind of people we need to impress – the commuters on my
train home to Sussex.

(Just to digress for a mo, isn't it time we knocked 'The
Man on the Clapham Omnibus' on the head as an arbiter of
public opinion? Very Old Labour, very Walworth Road. And
also very inaccurate. I tried to catch a bus the other day
when there was a delay at Vauxhall (the station was being
renamed 'Daewoo' under the new PFI arrangements). You
wait for twenty minutes and then half a dozen multi-
coloured fairground attractions arrive at once, all jostling
for the same stop. There's no need to remind everybody of
the transport situation in London, unless we're having a go
at the Mayor, so 'The Commuter on the Haywards Heath
Sprinter' would be my recommendation).

Anyway, Jane Asher – nice person, not a bad actress
and scrummy yet tooth-kind cakes, I'm sure. But you know
she's married to that horrible Sunday Times cartoonist,
don't you? He's got it in for you all right, scratching away
in his big house in Chelsea, photogenic kids, all the bloody
advantages that come from knocking the establishment.

You can't have forgotten the one he did after the fuel

crisis, that petrol pump with sticking-out ears and a mad grin and the last drops of petrol dribbling out of its limp hosepipe? (labelled 'Public Support' in case anyone had missed the point). The original's up on the wall in Gordon's bathroom if you need to be reminded.

2) The People's Cake. Hmmm. I wonder whether we aren't overdoing this 'people' bit. It has a whiff of Diana's funeral, do you know what I mean? Who was it said you can't please all of the people all of the time? Abraham Lincoln was it? On the money there, Abe baby. Sure, we're back in for another four or five years now, but that's a short time in politics as one of your other predecessors said, and it's never too early to start planning for the third term.

Let's keep our eye on the ball as far as this cake is concerned. What is it? It's a loyal gesture. I pride myself on being one loyal lady, and so are the commuters I share my train with. They're also almost exclusively Daily Mail readers. Okay, right now the Mail hates you and your wife and family and they'd hate your pets if you had any (they already suspect Cherie of killing the Downing Street cat). But there's nothing like having them inside the tent p*ssing out, instead of outside p*ssing in, is there? And you've got practically every other newspaper – Murdoch, Dirty Desmond etc – already inside p*ssing out, everybody except the Telegraph, and their readers will soon be too old to p*ss without a catheter.

So what about a competition in the Mail's Femail section to come up with the best recipe? I'll deal. I still play squash now and then with Lynda Lee-Potter, though these days she lifts her racquet less often than her face (miaow, stop it Anji!)

3) Your tie. I know it's a gesture of support for your buddy President Bush, who seems to have the secrets of the Universe as far as you're concerned right now, but I have to say I find the smoking Twin Towers motif a bit tacky. I'm sending a few more suitable ones round in a jiffy bag.

Sorry about the fag-ash. Can we do this on the mobile next time?

Date 25/10/01
From: Jo Moore
To: Martin Sixsmith

Hi Martin

I know I promised not to send any more e-mails, on pain of lingering death, but something happened to me this morning which got me a bit scared, and I thought I'd pass it on to you not only as my superior but also as I now see, a far wiser head than mine.

I was on the Underground travelling on the Victoria line on my way into work. A man of Muslim fundamentalist appearance got off the train at Daewoo and I noticed that he had left his bag behind. I grabbed the bag and ran after him, caught up with him at the top of the escalator and handed him back his bag. He was extremely grateful to me and reached into his bag which appeared to contain large bundles of banknotes. He offered me a reward, but obviously I refused in view of the events of September 11.

So he looked round, made sure nobody was watching and whispered to me: "I can never repay your kindness, beautiful lady, but let me try to with a word of advice. If you know anybody in a position of authority, anyone at all, tell them to stay out of central London this weekend". And with that he was gone.

Do you think we should do something? I'm frightened.

Apprehensively,
Jo

Date: 25/10/01
From: Martin Sixsmith [DOCDOT]
To: Jo Moore

Dear Jo
It was very sensible of you to alert me to this
possible situation.

I will certainly pass it on to Steve Byers. It
may be nothing, but better safe than sorry is my
motto, and as such it's been a trusted friend
throughout my career both at the BBC and now here
as DOCDOT.

Have a nice weekend, and don't worry that pretty
little head any more.

Martin Sixsmith [DOCDOT]

TRANSCRIPT OF CABINET MEETING

26 October 2001

CABINET SECRETARY (SIR RICHARD WILSON): Apologies have been received from the following: the Deputy Prime Minister, the Foreign Secretary, the Home Secretary, the Defence Secretary, the Minister for Trade and Industry, the President of the Council, the Minister for Overseas Development who adds that she's particularly unhappy not to be here...

THE PRIME MINISTER: Might it not be quicker to say who *is* present?

CABINET SECRETARY: The Prime Minister, the Chancellor of the Exchequer and the Secretary of State for Transport.

THE PRIME MINISTER: On the disappointing side. Where are they all?

THE CHANCELLOR OF THE EXCHEQUER (RT. HON GORDON BROWN): All spending more time with their constituents, for some reason.

THE SECRETARY OF STATE FOR TRANSPORT (RT. HON STEPHEN BYERS): Well don't look at me. I said don't look at me! It's not my fault. I was acting in good faith after being given misleading information by my civil servants about a possible terrorist attack.

BROWN: It was a practical joke. Charlie Whelan tried it out on me but you don't fool a son of the manse that easily.

THE PRIME MINISTER: You two are still in touch are you?

BROWN: It's a free country, isn't it?

THE PRIME MINISTER: You're right. Something else we've learned from the United States. Anyway it's very brave of you to stay in London Steve.

BROWN: Positively Queen Mother-like. Of course you could get to the East End in those days.

BYERS: I didn't want to miss anything that might turn out later to be important.

THE PRIME MINISTER: So Gordon, how's the Autumn Statement looking?

BROWN: That's for me to know and you to find out.

THE PRIME MINISTER: That's why I'm asking.

BROWN: I will shortly be putting the finishing touches to it. In the meantime I am compiling a portfolio of fiscally prudent measures, which taken together with the raft of...

THE PRIME MINISTER: Any room in that file for a cake?

BYERS: I'd like it to be noted that I laughed.

BROWN: I have repeatedly made it clear that there can be no frivolities such as cake until the relevant criteria are met.

THE PRIME MINISTER: Run them by me again will you?

BROWN: One – it doesn't cost us anything. Two – we don't have to pay anyone. Three – we will not be held responsible for its preparation or transportation. Four – we are not liable for any adverse after-effects. Five – it remains solely the property of Her Majesty's Government and any profits accruing from its sale or consumption will be paid directly to the Treasury. These strict conditions are to be implemented with immediate effect, and I commend them...

THE PRIME MINISTER: That doesn't rule out a competition, does it?

BROWN: Yes it most certainly does, because a competition means a prize, for which someone has to foot the bill. You've fallen at the first, as Robin Cook would say if he were here now and hadn't been so chicken.

THE PRIME MINISTER: 'Pussycat pussycat, where have you been...?'

BROWN: Now what?

THE PRIME MINISTER: It's something President Bush taught me. When confronted by a problem, revert to childhood. Richard, can you ask Alastair to get onto Black Rod and find out what the protocol is on meeting the Queen as a prize for the recipe we choose?

CABINET SECRETARY: Roger, Tony.

THE PRIME MINISTER: Sorry – Roger, can you…?

CABINET SECRETARY: I mean Roger as in 'Roger, willco'.

THE PRIME MINISTER: And how about – just bear with me here, I'm thinking on the hoof. 'Hoof!' – got it! How about as the runner-up's prize a day at the races with the Queen Mum, and third prize a weekend shooting endangered species with Prince Philip?

BYERS: We wouldn't want to offend the Prince of Wales. I've already had two letters from him this week complaining about car doors being slammed shut after midnight and planes interfering with his Channel 5 reception.

THE PRIME MINISTER: A day at Highgrove milling wheat? Dunno, I'd have to say the jury's still out on that one.

BROWN: It all sounds a bit gimmicky to me.

BYERS: Yes, what I made absolutely clear at the last cabinet meeting was we didn't want a gimmick. They kept on about it but I insisted.

CABINET SECRETARY: That's not what it says here.

BYERS: Then it's wrong.

THE PRIME MINISTER: Anyway, this isn't a gimmick. it's the chance for an ordinary loyal subject to meet his or her Queen. She's got lovely skin you know.

BYERS: I do know. I met her when I was escorting her onto the Royal Train. The operation passed without mishap, which underlines just how right I was to take Railtrack into Administr…

BROWN: I've been thinking about scrapping that train. If

they started using scheduled services the money saved would mean we'd only have to sell off the following school playing fields: Eton, Harrow, Charterhouse, Winchester...

THE PRIME MINISTER: Can we put all that on Hold for a bit, Gordon?

BROWN: Fine. I'll put it in the Pending Indefinitely tray with the Euro.

THE PRIME MINISTER: You know, I quite like these small Cabinet meetings. Anyone fancy nipping out to Starbucks?

CHAPTER FIVE

The Asian Babes in the Wood

"I T IS AN EXCEEDINGLY jolly top-hole place, Peter, don't you know – but when do we get to see Mister Blair?"

This was the moment Mandelson had been dreading. He had accomplished the first part of the plan without a hitch, getting the Hinduja Brothers kitted out in three identical sets of country-house weekend clothes in London's Jermyn Street. And then transporting them to Chequers in the heart of Buckinghamshire, a county synonymous with green leafiness but now a riot of autumnal red and gold as the seasons turned.

Enthusiastically the Indian businessmen had walked round the grounds, their individually monogrammed shooting sticks (SP, GP and PP) swishing through the crackling piles of pine cones, dead twigs and acorns. Politely they had toured the rooms of the house itself, admiring the portraits of past Prime Ministers who had lived, loved, relaxed, and played table tennis there. Now they wanted to see a real live one.

"How about a game of conkers? Can't pretend to be English if you don't play conkers!" said Mandelson, desperately looking at his New Statesman watch, a gift (officially a loan) from Geoffrey Robinson. It told the time in left-leaning countries throughout the world, and had also once chimed their national anthems, that was until the day it had been torn from Mandelson's wrist and thrown against a wall, after someone had forgotten to get the tarragon in the weekend shop.

"Enough games, Peter. As your vernacular so eloquently puts it – shit or get out of the pot".

The Hindujas were understandably impatient. They had prepared themselves for this most coveted of all invitations with the same assiduous attention to detail that made their business dealings a byword back in the subcontinent.

The night before they had even bought up all the seats at a Leicester Square cinema so that they could watch undisturbed a performance of 'Gosford Park'. They had pronounced it 'very good indeed, apart from the bit with Stephen Fry'.

"Maybe Mister Blair's body is in the library, stabbed in the back, just like in the movie?" joked Prakash ('PP') Hinduja.

"So who could possibly be a suspect?" wondered Gopichand ('GP') Hinduja.

"Or perhaps the solution is like Murder on the Orient Express, by your esteemed Agatha Christie" concluded Srichand ('SP') Hinduja, fixing Mandelson with a gimlet eye. "They all did it!"

It was high time to tell the truth and move on to the next stage of the plan. "The fact is, gentlemen", fessed up Mandelson, "That the Prime Minister isn't able to be here today. He sends profuse apologies and best wishes and hopes you'll understand".

"What precisely is it that we are meant to understand?" hissed SP Hinduja. "That our money is good enough but our presence is not?"

"We are the Untouchables now, is that it?" sneered PP Hinduja.

"I never said you were gangsters. That was Alastair Campbell" protested Mandelson.

Despite their obvious anger, the Hinduja brothers had to laugh. "You are holding the wrong end of the Penang Lawyer, my floppy-haired friend" said GP.

"I feel we are wasting our time, my brothers", said SP. "This man is – how does the expression go? – all mouth and no trousers. It was just the same when he said he would introduce us to the Bilderberg Group, the secret rulers of the world's economies".

"That's not fair!", spluttered Mandelson, now feeling he was being beaten up by a trio of thugees, albeit thugees wearing plus-fours, tartan socks and highly-polished brogues. "I really tried hard. Anyway, I got you in to see the Bootleg Bilderbergs, didn't I? They're just as good. You'd never have realised that wasn't the real Henry Kissinger if he hadn't stood up".

"Nevertheless, we are achieving nothing here. Please re-summon the limo".

"No no – look, I'm authorised to say that Tony really does want to do business with you", said Mandelson, his eyes scanning the room for the door that was a dummy bookcase, his escape route in case things turned really ugly.

"And yet he is not here. Somewhat like the dog that did not bark in the night", said SP.

"I too noticed something suspicious during our tour of the house" added GP. "The silk churidar kameez costing £1000 that we presented to Mister Blair's charming wife Cherie was hanging on the washing line outside the back door.

"And it was still dripping", added PP. "The mysteriousfulness is terrific".

"The thing is", said Mandelson, "Ever since the Bernie Eccleston and the Geoffrey Robinson affairs, the Prime Minister's decided he has to put a bit of distance between himself and chaps with lots of lolly such as yourselves, however excellent their company and welcome their donations. It's nothing personal".

"How much distance?" asked SP.

"About 300 miles I'd say" answered Mandelson. "They've gone up to Liverpool today, because the children have never met their maternal grandfather".

"Ah, Tony Booth, the celebrated Scouse Git from 'Death Till Us Part Do'" chuckled PP.

No no – it is 'Part Death Us Do Till' corrected GP. "Up the Hammers, you silly mare, old boy!"

"Anyway" said Mandelson, "The other day Channel 4 started showing the 'Confessions' films from the 70s as part of their 'Best of British' series and the cat was out of the bag. So that's where they are, on a family visit. But the important thing is that I'm here and you're here and I'm jolly well not going to let you leave until I've told you about this big cake we're planning for the Jubilee and got your creative and dare I say financial input on it!"

"Let us just huddle for a moment" said SP.

"Huddle away" said Mandelson, starting to feel confident he had reeled them in. "No pressure. I'll ring for some refreshments".

"Tiffin would be a delightful idea", said SP as the Hindujas came out of their huddle. "Let us sit down".

"Excellent!" said Mandelson, clapping his no-longer shaking hands. There would be no dead body found in the library *that* night. "But, erm – a word to the wise. Please don't put your shooting sticks in the carpet…"

As dawn stole across the Chiltern horizon the following morning, Peter Mandelson rose from the Chesterfield on which 100 years ago his great-grandfather Benjamin Disraeli had written his best-selling novels. He yawned, stretched and put a cheque for a million pounds into his back pocket.

"Just one item of small print, Peter" said Srichand Hinduja. "Why does it have to be a traditional English cake? If we are to invest in this item of confectionery cannot we have some say in its composition?"

"Let's discuss that over breakfast", said Mandelson. "How about some kedgeree?"

"Why not?" said Prakash. "After all, we did introduce it to your country".

"But *this* is our country" pointed out Gopichand. "Would you like to see my British passport?"

The Hinduja trio laughed, and after a moment Peter Mandelson laughed with them.

Daily Mail

From: Editor, Picture Desk
To: All Staff & Freelance Photographers
Date: 7/11/01

You may have heard that the plan to run a Jubilee Cake competition in Femail has been scuppered after the Prime Minister's wife decided, on a girly whim, that the people of Liverpool should be given the chance to plan and bake the cake as a way of boosting the city's economy. It seems that all the flowers from the Festival Gardens that were planted under Michael Heseltine's 1981 initiative have either died, or been stolen or smoked.

As you might imagine, the Editor is not taking this lying down, and has requested that we put Mrs Blair on 24-hour surveillance. This is to ensure we don't miss the kind of photo-opportunity that some of our rivals got after the 1997 election, ie Cherie at the front door of her Islington mansion in her nightie with her hair looking like a rat's nest.

A bonus system will be in operation for the duration of this campaign. Extra payments will be as follows:

Rat's nest hair: £75
Wearing something unflattering (eg mini-skirt, sari, hard-hat, Marge Simpson mask, Judge's wig): £100
Wearing Judge's wig and chewing the end of it: £150
Unnoticed sick on shoulder from Leo: £200
Unnoticed sick on shoulder from Euan: £250
Mouth open: £200
Mouth open, staring eyes: £250
Food round mouth: £500
Anything with Cruella de Vil caption potential: £750
Standing laughing over freshly-dug pet's grave: £10,000 and top-of-range Toyota

Happy snapping!

The Forecourt (formerly Third Way Vista)
Newick,
East Sussex.

8th November 2001

Dear Tony,

Please accept this as a formal letter of resignation. In three months' time I will be taking up the position of Director of Communications of BP, a company which henceforth has my complete loyalty, dedication and discretion. Virtues I happen to believe in. Old-fashioned of me maybe, but I'm stuck with it, so sorry and all that.

Why three months? you might be asking, assuming you – or whoever's reading your mail these days – get beyond the word 'resignation'.

It's known as a 'cooling-off period' Tony, and boy do I need to cool off. You wouldn't listen to me, would you? Instead you listen to your clever wife, QC, and what happens? You alienate the Daily Mail.

So what? you might say. They're never going to vote for me anyway, so who cares? Let me put it gently. I bet there isn't a pervert on a Portsmouth sink estate who would rather be in your shoes right now. They ain't gonna let you get away with it, baby.

Oh yes, those shoes. I'm afraid that a man nudging fifty who's thinning on top only draws attention to his age if he persists in sauntering about in no socks and canvas Docksiders. At least you know where you are with Gordon Brown when you see those black toe-caps trudging up Downing Street, making their stolid way inexorably towards Number 10. Just a tip sweetie!

Hugs, and a big sloppy kiss (the one you didn't get when we were 17)

Anji (Hunter)

[Editorial from **The Sun**, 18th November 2001]

John, Paul, George ...
And Thicko!

It's official, folks! The people of Liverpool really are more stupid than the rest of us!

It's a story that CAKES you cry for MERSEY. After a recent visit by Tony and Cherie Blair, the powers-that-be decided to give the Scousers the PLUM job of baking the Jubilee Cake.

But what do the bone-idle scallies do when handed this cash-for-work opportunity ON A PLATE? They don't BEATLE off to the larder and get out the eggs and flour like the rest of us would. No, they start having commiTEA meetings about exactly what kind of cake it should be. You couldn't CAKE it up!

When they were told they could CAKE anything that took their FANCY, just as long as it had a lot of tiers, would you believe the BIRKENHEAD-cases got hold of the wrong end of the SPOON and spent the rest of the week weeping buckets of TEARS instead and sticking teddy bears on railings, which is what passes for skilled work up there. And now they've taken the hump and are PUDDING out of the whole thing!

What a CAKE-up! But what do you expect from people whose idea of an inside lavatory is peeing through a rolled-up copy of the Daily Mirror! Obviously they were WACKED over the head a bit too much as kids!

The Sun says: now's the time to put a bomb under the M61 and float the whole of Merseyside back to Ireland where it belongs. BATTENBERGER off you Brookie barm-pots – we'd be a lot BUTTER off without you!

PRIME MINISTER
THE PRIME MINISTER WAS ASKED—

ENGAGEMENTS

Q1. [59803] Matthew Green (Ludlow): If he will list his official engagements for Wednesday 21st November.

The Prime Minister (Mr. Tony Blair): Dunno really – hadn't thought much beyond what I'd do once I got this far. Might have a cuppa, if somebody wouldn't mind directing me to the Members' Tea Rooms?

Iain Duncan Smith (Chingford and Woodford Green): No doubt the Prime Minister will note that there is a wide variety of cake which may be purchased in the Tea Rooms? *[Laughter]*

The Prime Minister: Good, because I'm a bit peckish.

Mr. Duncan Smith: Cake which is not only delicious but tangible – unlike I suspect the Jubilee Cake of which there is so far neither hide nor hair. Could the Prime Minister inform the House as to the progress of this mysterious delicacy?

The Prime Minister: You tell me. *[Cries of 'Oh']*

Mr. Duncan Smith: In fact isn't it true to say that we are as likely to see this cake as we are to find turkeys voting for deckchairs to be rearranged on the Titanic at Christmas?

The Prime Minister: Eh?

Mr. Duncan Smith: So would the Prime Minister have any objections if we on this side of the house planned our own Jubilee Cake and what's more made a darn sight better job of it?

The Prime Minister: None whatsoever, Clancy. Hope that cough clears up in time for Chrissy.

Charles Kennedy (Ross, Skye and Inverness): Wake me up before you go-go, don't leave me hanging on like a yo-yo…

Mr. Speaker: Order. That is not a question.

Mr. Kennedy: Fair enough – how about Whaddya wanna make those eyes at me for…?

The Prime Minister: You're drunk, you.

Mr. Kennedy: Ah yes, but as that great Liberal Democrat Winston Churchill might have put it – tomorrow I'll be drunk again, but you'll still be Prime Minister!

Mr. Duncan Smith: Point of Order, Mr Speaker – I don't think that *is* the Prime Minister.

The Prime Minister: Never said I was.

Mr. Duncan Smith: So who are you?

Mr. Speaker: Order. That question must be addressed through the Speaker.

Mr. Duncan Smith: Who is he, Mr Speaker? *[Cries of 'Who? Who?']*

Dennis Skinner (Bolsover): I know who it is – it's that bloke who got onto the Manchester United team photo and walked out at Lord's pretending to be an England batsman.

Not The Prime Minister: It's a fair cop. I'd just like to take this opportunity of saying Hello Mum!

Hon. Members: I spy strangers!

Mr Skinner: I tell you what – he talks a lot of common sense this fella, more than the Prime Minister does when he isn't swanning off round the world. Can we keep him?

Mr Speaker: Order.

Tam Dalyell (Linlithgow, Father of the House of Commons): I demand the immediate recall of Parliament!

CHAPTER SIX

Stormclouds Gather over M&S

"**J**o! jo!"

Work had finished for the day at the Department of Transport. Most of the department's vast staff had headed home into the winter evening, leaving only the office cleaners to move between the desks collecting up papers from waste-baskets, and deciding what could be leaked and what was to be shredded.

Martin Sixsmith left his Director of Communications suite, locked the door and for extra security bent down to insert a sliver of paper in the jamb at the bottom of the door, something he'd seen Robert Redford do in the movie 'The Sting'. And the similarity doesn't end there, thought Sixsmith to himself, winking roguishly as he caught sight of his reflection in a glass partition.

It was then he also saw Jo Moore, the Special Adviser to his boss Stephen Byers, fastening the luminous yellow cycling strips onto her jacket as she walked past the lifts with their 'Out of Order' signs and doors gaping open. The lifts hadn't worked for months, despite repeated phone-calls and faxes and the informal offer of peerages to the board of Dunkwerts, the company responsible for office maintenance.

It was just one of many not-so petty irritations Sixsmith had found since taking on this job. But foremost among them was walking down the stairs in front of him right now. It was time to nip this pretty but dangerous thorn in his side in the bud.

"Jo! Jo!" Sixsmith called her again. Moore didn't turn round, and Sixsmith was mentally composing a memo reprimanding her for insubordination, when he saw she was carrying a Walkman velcroed to one of her elbow-pads and was wearing headphones.

Sixsmith hurried past her, turned, waved and smiled. Moore brushed aside a brunette curl and removed one of her earpieces. She didn't stop walking.

"Good night, DOCDOT".

"Call me DOC – or better still, Marty"

"Whatever", said Moore. Sixsmith wasn't deterred. He had been the BBC's Moscow correspondent and could cope with freezing temperatures.

"What are you listening to?" said Sixsmith conversationally. "I'm a bit of a Dire Straits man myself. Used to be, anyway. Personally I don't think they ever again scaled the heights of Brothers in Arms…"

"It's one of Steve's speeches to the House of Commons", said Moore. "After he placed Railtrack in Administration".

"The Boss's Greatest Hits, eh?" joked Sixsmith, though inwardly he was shivering slightly at this display of dedication to the Minister. "Some people might think listening to that other Boss – Bruce Springsteen – at the end of a busy day might be a bit more relaxing…"

"Was there anything else, Marty?"

There was, and it was time to grasp the nettle. But just as he was opening his mouth to speak Sixsmith felt a jolt of static electricity from the stair railing shoot up his arm.

"Ouch! You know, there should be some way we can harness this static and maybe hook it up to the power supply. That might get the lifts working again".

"Look – I don't want to get out there and find my bike up on bricks, so…"

"Okay – I'll cut to the chase" said Sixsmith smoothly. "It's not exactly a secret, is it, that you and I haven't got off to a very good start, have we". Seeing he now had Moore's full attention as she took the other earpiece out of her ear, Sixsmith ploughed on. "Well, there might be a way we can both turn this to our advantage".

"Why, are you leaving?" said Moore. "Steve never said anything to me about this".

"Hold those horses, Jo!" laughed Sixsmith. "I don't know if you know this, but I used to work for the BBC. Well I've still got a lot of good friends there, and one of them has approached me about doing a new reality TV show, fly-on-the-wall sort of thing about this department. Working title 'The Secret Life of the Office'.

"Be a bit stupid calling it that", said Moore – "There's nothing secret about anything that goes on in the DOT".

"Ha! Nice one. They're all the rage now apparently – driving instructors, airport staff, Royal Opera House. And what's more they often make big TV stars out of completely ordinary people. You could be the next Carol Vorderman! What do you think?"

"You've missed something", said Moore.

"Payment? Well, I think our terms of employment might not permit…"

"Not you – her" said Moore, pointing to a matronly black cleaner on the stairs who was having difficulty bending down to pick up a discarded Twix wrapper.

"I'll do this for you this once, Alma" said Moore, reading the woman's name badge as she picked up the wrapper and put it in the black rubbish sack. "But any more oversights and it's deportation with no appeal, okay love?"

"You see, Jo?" said Sixsmith. "That's just the sort of thing that would endear you to millions. So, are you interested?"

They were now in the lobby and Moore put her helmet on as they made for the front doors.

"Steve would have to sanction it of course".

"Not necessarily. They can do amazing things with

hidden cameras these days. And he's got enough to worry about, what with the railways, and the buses, and the air traffic controllers, and the part-privatisation of the London Underground...and having to defend his decision not to fire you in the face of widespread public condemnation and calls for his own resignation...".

This last bit was for his own amusement, as by now Moore had left the building and as Sixsmith stood and watched, got onto her bike and rode off into the darkness.

Something was wrong with that picture. It nagged away at Martin Sixsmith like the gusts of sleety rain that caused him to turn his collar up against the bitter November night.

That's what it was – when Jo Moore had fed him the duff information about the non-existent terrorist attack, she said she'd come in to work on the tube.

Why hadn't she cycled as per usual? Was it a puncture? Had it been raining that morning? Or – and at this Sixsmith's BBC newshound's antennae, never far beneath the surface, bristled – was DOCDOT the one who was being set up?

Welcome to the Diary of
Kerry (The Vampire Slayer!)

By the blood of Zeus and the bones of my ancestral parents Atrius and Cyrene (Joyce to you!) Can it truly be that Kerry your humble scribe and chronicler of the bloody deeds that daily befall the worn-torn village of Amphipolis (Berkhamsted) is to be whisked away from her menial serf's job at Waitrose and sent to study among the ivory tusks of Oxford University?

You betcha! It transpires oh my subjects that I am to be the first wench bearing my name to go to university in a thousand generations of years of trying! The missive was conveyed on the winged heels of Mercury, actually a postman in blue shorts and white socks on a bike, why do they make them dress like that in the winter, my Mum says, no wonder they're losing millions.

But what heed need I pay now to the ramblings of the village soothsayer? It's on my conquests I am bound, and maybe at Oxford the elders there will vouchsafe me the secrets of the Ixion Stone, which gives great power to whomever uses it to transform themselves into the leader of all the centaurs. Or Media Studies would do. Who knows what this could lead to? A job in TV co-presenting Robot Wars? The sky — where the ancient Gods sit on high in marble armchairs, looking down with favour on their chosen daughter — is the limit!

And it's only ten days before the end of term, when Kerry will return in triumph to celebrate with her kinfolk the great pagan festival of Christmas! But they said don't worry that you've missed a few weeks. The Master will make sure you catch up. Wicked — if they've got the top guy from Doctor Who there it must be okay!

Gotta go, gotta retune my mobe so it plays something by Atomic Kitten. They went to college too!

TRANSCRIPT OF CABINET MEETING

22 November 2001

THE DEPUTY PRIME MINISTER (RT. HON JOHN PRESCOTT): On behalf of the Cabinet, may I say welcome back from Washington, Tony.

THE PRIME MINISTER: You may. First I'd like to assure you all that this is really me! What happened to the impostor, by the way?

PRESIDENT OF THE COUNCIL & LEADER OF THE HOUSE OF COMMONS (RT. HON ROBIN COOK): The last I heard he was in the Tea-Room, trying to persuade back-benchers that the Prime Minister hasn't forgotten them.

THE PRIME MINISTER: Persuading the who? Sorry Margaret, that's your line isn't it.

SECRETARY OF STATE FOR ENVIRONMENT, FOOD & RURAL AFFAIRS (RT. HON MARGARET BECKETT): I dare say I might have said it in the past. Since then I've been on an extensive fact-finding caravanning mission, and I'm now confident I'll be able to punch above my weight.

THE PRIME MINISTER: Hot dog! Before we leave the subject of Mini-Me, I wonder if it wouldn't, y'know, be a good idea if the guy carried on being a stand-in when I'm somewhere else in the world, like Afghanistan or upstairs with the family. I sometimes wonder if it's necessary for me to appear in the Commons at all.

SECRETARY OF STATE FOR TRANSPORT (RT. HON STEPHEN BYERS): Good point. Could I borrow him occasionally too? Say this afternoon?

PRESCOTT: Actually Tony, we've got someone who does that standing-in job already. Some might say he does it pretty capably.

THE PRIME MINISTER: Really, who?

PRESCOTT: Mister Blobby, who do you bloody think?

THE PRIME MINISTER: No, seriously, who is it?

COOK: Perhaps the Deputy Prime Minister would like to kick-off Senior Ministers' reports about what's been happening while The Prime Minister was abroad baby-sitting the Foreign Secretary.

SECRETARY OF STATE FOR FOREIGN AND COMMONWEALTH AFFAIRS (RT.HON JACK STRAW): Let it go, Robin.

COOK: Sorry, of course I meant accompanying the Foreign Secretary...on the piano, while he played the Israeli National Anthem on a jew's harp.

STRAW: You're a dirty shagger.

COOK: Yeah? Well your family's not just dysfunctional, it's a crime wave. Talk about The Sopranos!

MINISTER WITHOUT PORTFOLIO AND PARTY CHAIR (RT.HON CHARLES CLARKE): I'll come over there and knock both your heads together in a minute.

THE PRIME MINISTER: I dunno, you go away for a couple of months... Come on, guys – I've never known an atmosphere as poisonous as this.

CABINET SECRETARY (SIR RICHARD WILSON): Yes you have – Derry Irvine and Donald Dewar. And they had Stanley knives.

THE PRIME MINISTER: Anyway, Reports please.

PRESCOTT: Well the media still seem totally obsessed by this Jubilee Cake, so in your absence I've instructed the various interested departments to expedite this possible scenario...

THE PRIME MINISTER: And head 'em off at the pass?

PRESCOTT: If you like.

SECRETARY OF STATE FOR TRADE AND INDUSTRY (RT. HON PATRICIA HEWITT): I've received representations from various relevant companies eager to contribute their products for nothing, which I find heartening and something of a tribute to what I might call our grown-up approach to big business. To date they include HenCom — which you may remember was the Egg Marketing Board in the bad old days — The Jam Today Consortium and the Caster and Pollux Sugar Corporation.

PRESCOTT: This is assuming we're going down the jam sponge route. Margaret I think you've got some additional information from the cream arena?

BECKETT: I've been talking to dairy farmers. Discussions are at a sensitive juncture as details of the compensation package are still being hammered out by my civil servants. My most recent information suggests that we're still at the 'It's not enough' stage, but in my experience it never is, so I'm hopeful.

PRESCOTT: Why do they need compensation if they're giving the stuff for free?

SECRETARY OF STATE FOR CULTURE, MEDIA AND SPORT (RT. HON TESSA JOWELL): If I can just come in here — I've persuaded the ITV companies and Channel 4 to suspend their daytime transmission of adverts for compensation-claim companies between now and next summer.

STRAW: Well done Tessa. That sort of thing not only discourages people from standing on their own two feet, it makes them think there's something to be gained from only having one.

SECRETARY OF STATE FOR THE HOME DEPARTMENT (RT. HON DAVID BLUNKETT): Hang on, I thought I was the Home Secretary.

BYERS: Personally I find the 'blame culture' one of the least attractive features of this country.

CLARKE: Just to get back to the cake, I should add that Lord Sainsbury and Lord Haskins have both agreed to devote shelf space in their supermarket chains to the free ingredients. They'll be featuring it as part of their Christmas promotions and I hope one happy side-effect of this would be to blow Delia and her bloody cranberries right out of the water.

SECRETARY OF STATE FOR DEFENCE (RT. HON GEOFF HOON): On the subject of military actions, my department has been in discussion with various African nations re the possibility of sending us their entire output of dried fruit in exchange for top-of-the-range missile systems.

PRESCOTT: What do you have to say about that, Clare?

SECRETARY OF STATE FOR INTERNATIONAL DEVELOP-MENT (RT. HON CLARE SHORT): If it's a one-off, and it helps the economy of the poorest African countries ...then I'm prepared to be not totally unhappy.

CLARKE: We mustn't forget that the Tories have stolen our thunder and are planning their own Jubilee Cake – though I think we can safely disregard the Lib Dems' so-called Flapjack Initiative.

PRESCOTT: Can we?

CLARKE: We did a bit of research and found that a large part of the voting population resents the flapjack on account of having to spend £2.50 for them at railway stations when there's nothing else available.

BYERS: I hope nobody's going to blame me for that.

CLARKE: But as regards the Tories, they do seem to be mobilising a groundswell of anti-Government feeling.

PRESCOTT: Can we quantify this groundswell?

CLARKE: At the last count they've got the Women's Institutes on board, fuel protestors, farmers, teachers, policemen, doctors, nurses, patients in hospital corridors, bed-and-breakfast owners, greengrocers, asylum seekers, people who might have to live next to asylum seekers... They've gone so far as to track down all those punters who left flowers outside Kensington Palace when Diana died.

THE PRIME MINISTER: Now that's playing dirty pool. Who does that leave?

CLARKE: Everyone who voted for us at the last election, I suppose. We've got a majority of 170-odd, there must be a few of them out there somewhere.

SECRETARY OF STATE FOR EDUCATION AND SKILLS (RT. HON ESTELLE MORRIS): On a brighter note, Tony, when we heard that the Tories were using a recipe provided by the Hemel Hempstead WI, we looked into their members' family circumstances, and I'm pleased to report that we've been able to regrade their kids' A-level results and fast-track them into places at Oxford, under the Chancellor's anti-elitism quota system.

THE CHANCELLOR OF THE EXCHEQUER (RT. HON GORDON BROWN): I'll be monitoring their expenditure closely for any imprudence, and in due course for signs of a return on our investment at the ballot box.

COOK: That's not a bad idea, Estelle – get 'em while they're young. Why don't we try using the Blue Peter Christmas Appeal?

STRAW: You just want to get a grip on Konni Huq, shagger.

PRESCOTT: So what about recruiting Labour voters?

BYERS: Can we trust them? What do you think, Tony?

THE PRIME MINISTER: Guys, don't think I don't appreciate all the hard work you've put into this. I really do. But there is a Third Way.

BLUNKETT: Oh-oh.

SHORT: Unhappy again. Sorry folks.

►●◄
three guys in bow-ties!
public relations

Marjorie Mowlam,
Secretary of State for Northern Ireland (?)
Stormont is it,
Northern Ireland.
UK is it.

12th December 2001

Hi Mo,

Hope this reaches you okay, we forgot to grab the contacts book when we left – in a rather indecent haste! –
our last agency (Jesus Mary Bogle Joseph).

Any road up – what seems like eons ago now you contacted us about doing some PR for you if and when the
situation arose. You'd just had some kind of barney with
the Rev. Ian Paisley, tearing him off a strip for persist-
ently referring to the Pope as 'His Satanic Majesty the
red-socked Antichrist' and were worried you might be in
for some official kneecapping (yikes!).

We've followed your subs. career with interest Mo, but it
strikes Jake, Gadge and me that you might be in the market (filthy commercial phrase!) for a bit of professional
help again. We've done successful image rebranding for
clients both big (Consignia, used to be the terminally
dull old Royal Mail) and small who intend to be ginormous (The Friday People literary agency). In the inter-

vening period since we last shot paintballs at each other on the Peace Process Bonding Weekend, we've built up something of a rep for specialising in successful placement for pols such as yourself who want to repackage.

Did you see that blonde bombshell on the Brian Conley Show at the weekend, dressed to kill in denim and plugging her newest raunchy nov? Sure, Annie Widdecombe's nose-stud was only stick-on, but appearances count for everything Mo and we're very pleased that The New-Look Widdster was our doing.

A glance at the publishers' catalogues for next spring tells me that you've got an autobiography coming out. Great. It'll be huge of course but wouldn't it be even more of a cert if you could give the book a nudge in the right public-awareness direction, eg plugging it on the Graham Norton Show? You could produce a special pop-up edition, open it and out would shoot (for the sake of argument) a giant dildo, right in Graham's face! Tacky you might think, and you'd be right, but let's wait till you see the first week's sales figures before you get into too condemnatory mode!

We'd also be looking to getting you a regular judge's berth on the next series of Pop Stars and Pop Idol – but most crucial of all Mo, is to land yourself a sit-com. It's rapidly becoming a must-do for A-list celebs, and we'd be very surprised indeed if this time next year, Davina McColl and Johnny Vaughan weren't being mentioned in the same Legends of Comedy breath as Babs Windsor and Rik Mayall.

So I'm enclosing a tape of the Mary Tyler Moore show, circa the 70s which is certainly the hot decade as far as the current TV schedulers are concerned. Being able to name the firemen in 'Trumpton' practically guarantees you a prime-time Saturday night slot! Anyway, pay particular attention to the credits, where Mary stops in the middle of a New York street and hurls her hat into the air in a lovable, here-I-am-world way.

You've got lovability by the skip-load, Mo, so wouldn't it be just excellent if you were to stroll down Downing Street, thinking wistfully of what might have been, before you tear off that trademark wig of yours and toss it in a Mary-homage into the air in slow-motion?! Freeze Frame, Studio Audience Goes Ape-Shit. You'd have a full head of hair underneath of course, courtesy of studio make-up (or has it grown back since we last met?) so there'd be no problems about getting a pre-watershed slot.

Anyway, have a thinkington and get back to me when you're ready. We'll be having mince-pies here on the afternoon of the 18th (assuming we can work out the microwave!), so bop along why don't you.

Happy Crimble and here's to the Mo Show in 2002!

Bez Trux

MEMO

For: TB's eyes only

From: Alastair Campbell

Date 13/12/01

Subject: Ruining my Christmas

Not being a member of the Department of Transport, I feel free to commit my thoughts to paper.

You've done it again haven't you, you frigging control-freak. What the hell is a halwa and where did the idea come from?

I'm waiting.

AC

MEMO

For: TB's Eyes Only

From: Alastair Campbell

Date 14/12/01

Subject: Ruining My New Year Too

Thanks for the information about the Indian carrot cake. No answer to the second part of my question I note, which leads me to suspect that you've been talking to Mandelson again – how many times have I told you about hanging round with naughty boys?

The cuttings agency we use has also dug up something from the Leicester Mercury about Keith Vaz and his missis allegedly running a sweat-shop in the basement of the constituency office. Seems it's suddenly switched from producing Ali G in Da House t-shirts to a full-scale operation chopping up pistachios and blanched almonds.

And a million pounds has mysteriously appeared on our most recent bank statement. Is it being fanciful of me to detect a certain smell in this, ie the three competing after-shaves of our old friends the Hinduja Brothers?

Anyway, let's see how we can deal with this latest fine mess you've gotten me into (you know, sometimes I think I might as well go back to editing the Readers' Wives page in Forum, or the Daily Express as it is now).

The Hindujas'll want something big in return for their money, and my first thought was a joint honour, like when the whole of Malta was awarded the George Cross after the war (though I know they sent it back after you gave Tuscany their GC last year). But then I remembered seeing the framed photos on the Hindujas' mantelpiece that time

we celebrated Diwali at their Carlton House Terrace gaff –
when Prescott arrived on the two elephants. So it occurs to
me that they might be happy just to be snapped shaking
hands with the Queen, something to go in their Hall of Fame
alongside Mother Teresa and Lily Savage.

There might even be an advantage to be gained from
having a big ethnic cake, because I have to say I'm being
kept awake thinking how we can avoid a repetition of the
Dome's opening night balls-up. Remember the Queen standing there with that ploughed-field look on her face, taking
your hand during Auld Lang Syne like it had leprosy?

Apart from backing a winner, we know there's nothing
that gets the old girl going like a display of Commonwealth
dancing, so presenting the thing to her surrounded by
whirling dervishes might force her to crack a smile. I'll
check out if there are any Zulu musicals coming into the
West End, we could borrow some of their cast for the day.

Another thought: the Yanks are very big on carrot cake,
so maybe we can turn it into an Anglo-American gesture of
solidarity?

I understand the Cabinet's getting a bit arsey about having to devote so much time to these cake arrangements, so
my advice would be to form an inner circle that could meet
in the COBRA office while the War Cabinet breaks for lunch.

Hang on – I've just seen Mo Mowlam out in the street,
with a camera crew. What's she up to? Just going to look.

Bloody hell – now that's what I call semi-detached. Or
unhinged, more likely. Could be useful.

AC

*Season's Greetings from the Cook family
to all our friends!*

Well what a busy and topsy-turvy year it's been for the
Cooks and no mistake! Some of you living abroad or
without access to 'the media' might be wondering why
our card and annual newsletter hasn't been sent from the
Foreign and Commonwealth Office this year! Well the
fact is that in June Robin was given the most marvellous
new job as 'Leader of the House of Commons' as a
reward for everything he'd done for the previous administration.

'Leader' sounds very important, doesn't it, and it is –
though as Robin is the first one to point out, it doesn't
mean he's actually running the country. That task
remains in the very capable hands of Tony Blair – I know
he'd blush if he read this letter but he won't as he and
Cherie aren't getting one this year.

Leaving the Foreign Office was a bit of a wrench for
Robin, as over the last four years he'd visited so many different countries and enjoyed a wide variety of their cus-
toms (and local beverages!!) and made such a lot of
friends. Any day now the postman will be bringing a
whole sack full of Christmas cards from the four corners
of the globe which the Foreign Office hasn't got round to
forwarding yet (that place must just have fallen apart
when we left!)

But we have to move onward, or we get stale, don't we.
People say 'Goodness Gaynor, what are you going to do
with all those air-miles you must have totted up?' The
truth is I haven't decided yet, as my mind is still reeling

from the sights and sounds of the fabulous places I've visited with Robin and taken photographs of, from the Taj Mahal in India to the EEC headquarters in Brussels. It'll probably take me the whole of next year to sort out the albums – the photos currently reside in their Boots envelopes in a Waitrose 'Bag for Life' under the stairs, but I won't bore you with the details. Just watch this space!

Meanwhile there's a lot to be said for sitting at home watching the world go by, doing the crossword and writing the occasional 'spoof' letter to the agony aunt in one of the Sunday papers. Yes, you've guessed it it's Robin's 'ex', Margaret – oops, sorry, *Doctor* Margaret Cook, who manages to hang on to her job in Scotland as a glorified hospital porter while handing out advice to all and sundry on toy-boys (something she is an authority on) and spots. You might wonder how she manages to cram it all in, until you consider the amount of spare time she has on her hands now.

As for Robin's 'even better better half' as he calls me, I'd be rushed off my feet if I allowed it to, making sure Robin arrives properly briefed every day for another challenging session in the Commons. For example, did you know that 'filibuster' was originally a Dutch word which has the same origin as 'freebooter'? Lots of informative little snippets like that come my way, which prove invaluable when Robin is hosting a get-together of important sub-committee chairmen – and women! – and needs to break the ice before they get down to the vital business of the day planning who sits where, etc.

One project that we're both very much looking forward to in 2002 is the Jubilee Cake.

Not for the first time the Cabinet seems unable to agree on who should do what – Robin says it's like the euro referendum all over again! – but he's very determined that it should reflect the best of what the Labour Party stands for. Something for everybody in other words that's full of flavour and wholesome yet without having to be 100% good for you – he's not making that 'ethical' faux pas again!!

Some of the Cabinet have now gone into secret session to decide on exactly what sort of cake it should be, and of course Robin would have been invited to join them but quite frankly he's just too busy helping sort out MPs' holiday travel arrangements. But he did hear a whisper the other day and promptly went down to Ladbrokes to get the 12 to 1 available on a Rich Dundee Cake. Some things don't change!!

Our best wishes to you and yours for a Christmas and New Year that's as successful as ours continue to be.

Robin and Gaynor Cook

CHAPTER SEVEN

The Pretzelgate Conspiracy

P RESIDENT GEORGE W. BUSH strode into the James S. Brady Briefing Room in the West Wing of the White House. "Where's C.J.?" he barked.

The staff looked at each other and raised their eyebrows. At least Ronald Reagan genuinely couldn't remember their names. Bush thought it gave him what he liked to think of as 'prez-cred' to call them after the characters in what had become his number-one favourite TV show after the sports.

"I'm here, Mr President", said Press Secretary Ari Fleischer.

"Good. C'mon!"

And he was out of the door as Fleischer dropped his clipboard and hurried after the President. He caught up with his boss a dozen corridors later. Bush had studied tapes of 'The West Wing' closely, and had learned that the way to make policy was walking around at incredible speed, striding in and out of rooms as he greeted passing advisers.

"Hi Sam…how y' doing, Donna? You get those flowers from Josh?".

The staffers (who were called Phil and Hope) smiled and covered their White House badges. Unlike Gerald Ford, one of his predecessors in the Oval Office, Bush had mastered the art of walking and chewing gum at the same time, but there was no sense in confusing the President needlessly.

"Okay C.J.," said Bush over his shoulder to his panting communications supremo. "Here's what you put in your next press thing. You know if I spelt my first name with a 'J' instead of a 'G' I'd have the exact same initials as President Jed Bartlet? How about that?"

"Very interesting, Mr President" said Fleischer. "Your politics though are a tad different. And you don't suffer from MS".

"You're darn tootin', said Bush. "None of that Women's Lib horse feathers on my watch". They were now in the Oval Office, but no sooner had the President sat down behind his desk and swivelled, than he was off again, through the French windows onto the Terrace, past the Rose Garden, into the Roosevelt Room and out into the corridor where he finally paused by a water cooler.

"Something else you could help me with" said the President.

"Anything, Mr President - anything at all".

Bush looked at Fleischer through narrowed eyes. "Gee, C.J. – you swallowed a dictionary? What happened to 'Yeah' or 'Okay'?".

"Okay".

"Okay", said Bush, heading off in the direction of the Blue Room. "Now in the last segment I saw Toby Ziegler do sump'n I found real interesting".

"Yeah – was it when he warns President Bartlet not to invade a country just because its leader wears combat fatigues and a moustache? I gotta say I thought Toby was talking a lot of sense… "

"Will you pipe down, Mister? What he does, is throw a baseball against a wall, and catches it every time. I've re-run the tape again and again, and he hasn't missed the dadblamed thing once! How's Toby do that?"

"Digital enhancement, maybe?" ventured Fleischer "It is a television show".

"Okay, but Osama bin Laden don't know that" said

Bush. "Wouldn't it be just dandy to send a tape out to him in Afghastinan, kind of like a signal not to mess with us, because we're on target every time? Where the heck are we, C.J.?"

Just what I was wondering, thought Fleischer. Not on Planet Earth, that was for sure. But then he realised that he and the President had somehow wandered down several flights of stairs into the White House mail-room, where a young black intern was nervously holding a parcel.

"Sir, you're in the Mail-Room, Sir!" said the intern.

"You're a black fellow, aren't you?" said Bush, peering at him.

"Yes Mr President, Sir!"

"Shoot – I'm gonna call you Charlie! What you got there, Charlie?"

Bush reached for the parcel, but Fleischer intervened and took it first.

"Careful, Mr President – it could be Anthrax".

"It's from England, not Anthrax. You guys think I know squat about foreign countries! Look – there's Her Highness the Queen Majesty's head on the stamps".

President Bush eagerly opened the parcel. Inside was something wrapped in tin-foil, with a Post-It note adhering to the side.

"It's from my good friend Prime Minister Blair", said Bush, reading the note. "Says would I give this piece of carrot-cake the once-over and call him on the red phone with my opinion".

The cake sat plump and moist in its foil wrapping and looked too good to resist. Bush took a large bite as he set off rapidly up the stairs from the mail-room. But this was one more manoeuvre than even Gerald Ford had dared try – walking, chewing and climbing stairs simultaneously. Bush started to choke, staggered and grabbed for the stair-rail. Three secret servicemen guffawed at what they first thought was presidential horsing around, then hurried to surround him.

"Big Bird's Down!" they yelled urgently into their radios, even though they were within a few feet of each other.

"Quick! Go to commercial!" spluttered the President.

"Can't do that sir", said Fleischer, starting to sweat. This could be bigger than 9/11. Hell, it could even be a bigger deal than 7/11. "We have a situation here. Er, okay, yeah, let me think – yeah, okay – what would C.J. Cregg do?"

CHEQUERS

February 10th 2002

To (*in alphabetical order, so we don't have any
arguments*): Alastair C, Charlie F, Derry I, John B,
Peter M and Philip G,

Guys, I need you to help me here. The good news
is that President Bush's people are putting it out
that he choked on a pretzel, not the carrot-cake we
sent him, and there's also some wicked gossip that
he was actually in a bit of a Euan-in-Leicester-
Square state at the time, which I guess is spin working to our advantage for once!

It's an ill wind, because the Cabinet Secretary
has heard from Black Rod that the Queen Mother
is very partial to Rich Dundee Cake, and I'm not
minded to argue with that, especially in the present sad circumstances. While we're on that subject
(can you say that about the Queen's sister?) I know
it wouldn't be totally accurate to call Margaret the
People's Princess but I'm sure the guys at Formula
One and everyone associated with tobacco advertising will miss her.

But I'm afraid all the other vibes I'm picking up
are negative. Black Rod reports that the Queen
refuses point-blank to go to The Dome ever again.
Actually I don't think we'd ever suggested it as a
serious venue for the cutting presentation, she just
wants to have a gratuitous sideswipe at it. Latest
news from the focus groups is that apathy and dis-
trust of the govt is at an all-time high, with particular scorn reserved for The Cake. They don't believe
we can deliver, either tastily or on time. Well they're
wrong. Silvio Berlusconi rang me this weekend to
offer a giant pannatone as a gesture of support,
and I think we should have this standing by in

case of bad weather or union trouble, whatever. But in the meantime let's run with the Rich Dundee and try and whip up some public support now that we can legitimately say it's By Royal Appointment.

Especially as the Tories are still trying to steal our thunder with their Chocolate Gateau. I hear a rumour that they're planning to bring it into London on a big open truck pulled by the 'Hogwarts Express'. I'm simply at a loss to understand this if it turns out to be true - I thought the woman who writes the Harry Potter books was a single mother as well as a billionairess, an archetypal New Labour voter in other words?

So, Blue Sky Thinking Caps on, everybody, and let's get out there and sell our wares to Mr and Mrs Joe Public. Talking of partnerships, what do people think about me doing a specially-adapted fun duet with Elton John? ('Don't Go Baking My Tart' sort of thing, only with a more positive message?) Crap idea, or not? I'm just not sure anymore.

But look, I'm determined to make this thing happen, and not to have to create a diversion like bombing Iraq (the press would have a field day) or trying to ban fox-hunting again (The Field would have a press day).

T

PS: Peter, could you break the news to the Hinduja Brothers that we're not taking their cake any further. Apologise from me and say we'll make it up to them somehow - maybe we could give them the franchise to open an Indian restaurant in the House of Commons or something?

Department of Environment, Food and Rural Affairs

Vanessa Whitburn,
Editor, 'The Archers',
BBC, Pebble Mill,
Birmingham, B5 7QQ   11 February 2002

Dear Vanessa,

You no doubt remember the last successful collaboration between The Archers and this department (known as MAFF in those unenlightened days) during the so-called foot-and-mouth outbreak of 2001. You were good enough then to incorporate official government advice into the programme, which it's fair to say helped prevent what could have been a disaster for the 'farming community'. I think the moment when Ruth said "Ooh David, I'm sooo happy the crisis is officially ooover" after a fortnight had more national impact than any number of dusty and ruinously expensive government leaflets!

Well here's another chance to 'do your bit', this time for the upcoming Golden Jubilee. We know how loyal everyone in Ambridge is to the Royal Family, ever since HRH the late Princess Margaret made her guest appearance at Grey Gables with Jack Woolley (happily still with us!). I'm attaching the script of a scene that we would very much like to be recorded and used in the programme as soon as possible. As you'll see, it follows one of your current storylines, and hopefully the message will be picked up subliminally by your large audience!

Yours sincerely,

Margaret Beckett
(dictated by someone else and signed in her absence).

[TELEPHONE RINGS]

BRIAN ALDRIDGE: Brian Aldridge.

SIOBHAN HATHAWAY: Brian – it's me.

BRIAN: Oh hello.

SIOBHAN: Brian, I've got to see you!

JENNIFER ALDRIDGE: Who is it, darling?

BRIAN: It's nothing, Jenny – just estate business.

SIOBHAN: Is that how you think of me now, Brian? Estate business? Something to be bought and sold like a tithe barn?

BRIAN: Well you're certainly starting to look as big as a barn, ever since I got you pregnant!

SIOBHAN: Brian!!

JENNIFER: Brian??

BRIAN: Er, apparently there's a ewe pregnant again up on Lakey Hill.

JENNIFER: Well you can't do anything about it now, you're helping me make Ambridge's section of the Golden Jubilee Cake.

SIOBHAN: Brian I've got to see you this minute!

BRIAN: No can do I'm afraid. I'm just in the middle of weighing out sultanas.

SIOBHAN: Don't try and pull the wool over my eyes, Brian Aldridge. Everybody knows Stir-Up Sunday is in December. This is February.

BRIAN: I'm aware of that. But this is much more important than Christmas pudding. This Jubilee cake is our chance to help the government show Her Majesty just how grateful we are to her for the last 50 years. It really is all hands to the pump.

SIOBHAN: Don't talk to me about pumps. There's a big bun

in the oven here with your name on it.

BRIAN: Oh well, if that's your attitude...

SIOBHAN: Brian, I'm sorry. Look, Tim thinks I'm in Hamburg, so why don't we meet at the Moat House on the Felpersham Road...

BRIAN: I'd love to be there, I really would, but with less than four months to go till the Golden Jubilee, I've simply got to help get this cake ready!

JENNIFER: Brian, I need you for the lemon zest...

BRIAN: I'm sorry, I've got to go.

SIOBHAN: All right – will you think about me, just a little, while you're making the Jubilee Cake?

BRIAN: Of course – all the time.

SIOBHAN: How will you think about me?

BRIAN: Well, d'you remember when we saw that movie American Pie?

SIOBHAN: Ugh!

Date: 15th February 2002
From: Jo Moore
To: DOCDOT and the Department

Re: *The Hogwarts Express Journey (not!)*

Here's some good news I didn't want burying! The
Department, with the full backing of European Law,
can put the skids right under the Tories' publicity
stunt to use the Harry Potter train to promote
their cake! Apparently it's illegal to transport
perishable foodstuffs for long distances at high
speeds in the open air unless it's properly
strapped down (and wouldn't that make a mess of
their chocolate topping!) – risk of walnuts flying
off and decapitating kiddies etc.
Sorry Marty, I know HRH Princess Margaret's funeral
is today, but I couldn't wait to tell everybody!
Jo

From: DOCDOT
To: Jo Moore

My office. Now.

TRANSCRIPT OF BRIEFING GIVEN TO LOBBY JOURNALISTS

Government Spokesman: Just to clear something up from last week, and the ridiculous allegations, aka 'Garbagegate', that the Prime Minister was somehow putting pressure on his opposite number in Romania by promoting a Labour Party donor's attempt to buy their steel industry...

Man from Daily Telegraph: Never mind that. What about the Jo Moore and Martin Sixsmith resignations?

Woman from Daily Mail: Did he make a pass at her but the bitch turned him down?

Government Spokesman: ...I'm pleased to put your minds at rest by reassuring you that research into the workforce's ancestry reveals that not only can Mr Lakshmi Mittal's company call itself truly British, but also that all its employees are qualified to play cricket for England, and rugby for Wales...

Man from Sunday Times: Who came up with that factoid? Liar Byers?

Government Spokesman: Steve Byers continues to enjoy the full supp...

Woman from Daily Star: Was he jealous of the relationship between Jo Moore! Moore! and Sexy Sixsmith?

Man from Daily Express: Was it a love-rat triangle?

Man from Sunday Times: Will Liar Byers Pants-On-Fire quit now?

BBC Political Correspondent Andrew Marr: Would 'The Seventh Deadly Spin' be an admittedly flippant, but containing more than a grain of truth, way of describing...

Girl from ITN (shouting across road): Will the Prime Minister be resigning?

Government Spokesman: Yes.

Everybody: What?

MEMO

For: TB's Eyes Only
From: Alastair Campbell
Date: 21/2/02
Subject: The DOT Brouhaha

Sorry, I had to come up with something out there to buy us a bit of time. A little trick I've picked up from your precious Minister of Transport – say one load of bollocks then say a completely different load of bollocks a week later, so by the time they've gone back and checked their notes and the tapes everybody's bored with the bollocks anyway. Of course Byers can't get away with it forever – I'd give him another two months, which might work in our favour timing-wise.

We offered Martin Sixsmith the unique career opportunity (ahem) of moving sideways and helping organise the Jubilee celebrations, ie make him carry the can for the Cake. But now he's talking about entering the priesthood, live on TV, probably as a way of out-holier-than-thouing his old BBC mucker Martin Bell, so we've been obliged to offer him 'gardening leave'. I'd leave him in the bloody Downing Street garden all right, buried next to where Cherie's supposed to have stuck the cat.

And I hear he's sold his story to the Sunday Times. Whatever happened to good old-fashioned journalism, those innocent days of The Old Codgers and Cassandra and 'You are Chalky White and I claim my five pounds?' Now it's a case of 'You are Chalky White the paedophile, and I claim my five thousand pounds or else you'll get your house torched'. We're swimming with sharks my friend, and it's time we started fighting back.

First we need to get the editors on-side. Appealing to their vanity usually works, so I've drafted something. What do you think? Actually it doesn't matter what you think, it's been sent out already with the free gift. The cake's Mr Kipling by the way, and for security I had the original packaging put in black sacks and dumped in the river by the Thames Barrier, just in case that nonce who roots through famous people's bins and flogs the contents to the News of the Screws is sniffing around.

I also checked back and found that Mr Kipling doesn't actually exist, so we won't find ourselves in an embarrassing 'Lord Kipling' cash-for situation come June.

The things we do for love.

AC

From the Prime Minister

5 March 2002

Dear Charles Moore/Alan Rusbridger/Piers Morgan/David Yelland (etc),

As Editor of the Daily Telegraph/Guardian/ Mirror/Sun (etc) you are one of our most influential and valued friends.

We've been racking our brains over the last few years CHARLES/ALAN/ PIERS/ DAVID (etc) to think how we can best make amends for that grievous blow to your esteem you suffered on Millennium Eve, December 31st 1999. Remember how you and other important dignitaries – though naturally less important than yourself, CHARLES/ ALAN/ PIERS/ DAVID (etc) – were left waiting for twenty minutes on a cold station platform at Stratford with only a paper cup of non-vintage champagne for company? Not a good way to start the 21st century, a point you made forcibly in the Daily Telegraph/ Guardian/ Mirror/Sun (etc) – and you were right!

So please accept this gift-wrapped exclusive sample piece of Jubilee Cake as a small token of appreciation from the Prime Minister to you. Imagine the look of delight on the faces of the other members of the MOORE/ RUS-BRIDGER/ MORGAN/ YELLAND (etc) households as you show them your treasured possession this morning (or at the weekend if it's your turn to have the kids)!

And should you decide that it looks too good to eat, the eco-friendly stainless-steel style presentation pack, made at award-winning Romanian steel mills, will ensure the cake will stay fresh and ready to be admired by generations of MOORES/ RUSBRIDGERS/ MORGANS/ YELLANDS (etc) to come.

You have also been entered in a Free Prize Draw. The winner will get the chance to meet a member of the Royal Family (to be determined) at the presentation of the Jubilee Cake at a venue also to be arranged (but rest assured it won't be you-know-where!), date to be finalised.

Yours 'in the ink', and let our new motto be:
New Labour – New Friends!

Tony Blair

CHAPTER EIGHT

Political Awakenings

JOYCE HAD BEEN SO Looking forward to Kerry coming home. It had seemed a long time between Christmas and Easter – 'the Hilary Term' as Kerry had called it, flexing her newly developed vocabulary muscles. Oxford was having a dramatic effect on that girl, and not altogether for the better thought Joyce, as she moved aside the pile of heavyweight political biographies that threatened to overbalance the kitchen table.

But some things don't change that much, she added to herself as Kerry bounded in for breakfast, wearing the crotchless pyjamas she'd bought on the last school trip to Rhodes, and that familiar teenage look of disgust on her face.

"God, what's that chemical stink coming from the toaster?"

"Raspberry Pop-Tarts – your favourite".

"*Mum!!* Kill me now why don't you, before I've even had chance to sit Part One", sneered Kerry. "Do you know how many E numbers there are in there?"

"All right then – what about some Special K?"

"Special GM you mean. No way, I'll have one of these eggs, that is assuming they're free-range and not got by torture".

"Oh no you won't, young lady". The bowl of eggs was special too. In the secret arrangements for preparing the Conservative Party cake, each member of the WI had been allocated a task, to be undertaken on a certain day. Since the bitter disappointment of the Hogwarts Express, it had been decided that the ingredients would be taken down to London separately and assembled on the day of the presentation itself at a mystery location. Joyce had bought her eggs as per instructions and was leaving them at room temperature until the vital one-word order came through: beat.

"What's this RI:SE crap you're watching?" said Kerry, frowning at the small television set on the counter.

"It's the new breakfast show", said Joyce. "Lots of showbizzy items about people with only one name I've never heard of but you probably have, like Gareth and Darius".

"As if. What's the colon in the middle all about?"

"I don't know – you're the one at Oxford". Joyce couldn't resist it.

"Is it like Shi'ite, or something?"

"And we'll have less of that language while you're in my house, thank you very much".

Too late Joyce realised that she wasn't the only Te Kanawa woman spoiling for a fight that morning.

"Technically speaking it isn't your house", snapped back Kerry. "It's a council property which you bought at a giveaway price in the Thatcher era while hard-up families who can't afford to get a toe-hold on the property ladder have to live on top of each other in bed-and-breakfasts run by slum landlords".

Joyce opened and closed her mouth like Barry the goldfish in his bowl on the window-sill. The best she could come out with there and then was "If you can find a better hole, why don't you go to it".

It was as uneven a contest as a team of disabled no-hopers taking on Manchester United at full strength. Kerry's eyes welled up with tears that were 100% genuine and politically correct.

"That's not funny, Mum. It's what they say in the back streets of Rio de Janeiro, only there they mean it. Some people really do have to live in holes".

That was more than enough for Joyce. "I've never heard such a lot of claptrap. Somebody's been filling up your head with rubbish, some spotty boyfriend who thinks his half-baked ideas might get your knickers off and into bed. Who is it – this Gordon you keep ringing? Have you seen the size of your mobile phone bill?"

"That Gordon", said Kerry icily, "Just happens to be the Chancellor of the Exchequer. He's keeping an eye on my progress, making sure I don't fall in with the wrong crowd – la-di-da toffs only oot for a good time, as he puts it".

"Kerry, he's *married*", said Joyce, as gently as she could. "Or if he isn't he's gay, according to Sue Lawley on Desert Island Discs. Either way, he's leading you up the garden path".

"Something you know a bit about, right?" said Kerry, and then hurried to the toaster to rescue the Pop-Tarts which were sending a plume of acrid black smoke up to the ceiling as their innards imploded. She had broken a family taboo by referring to her long-gone father, and they both knew it.

The old Kerry would just have muttered a sullen apology and let it end there. But this was the newly-confident, exuberance of Oxbridge-youth Kerry. Recklessly she plunged into dangerous waters.

"What a sad old Tory story that was! At least you might have picked Cecil Parkinson or Jeffrey Archer, some sleazoid with a bit of cash. But you have to fall for the first sad bastard councillor who comes along, with his shiny-arsed suit and his golf and his Golf and his wife and two kids in…"

"I'm going out now" said Joyce quietly, taking a headscarf from the peg behind the back door. "Can you tape 'Simon Schama's Worst Plagues in History – Ever!' on BBC2 for me?"

"Sure, but – where will you be?" said Kerry, feeling suddenly lonely and not at all like a sophisticated eighteen-year old who could hardly wait to vote for the first time in the forthcoming local elections.

"The Post Office – the Quilters have raised money for a Loop-Link for deaf customers and I'm switching it on. Then tonight I've got tickets to see Danny la Rue in The Vagina Monologues at Tring. Don't wait up".

Duh, thought Kerry, as the door closed behind her mother. You bet I will. And so will Pete. The dog, who Kerry sometimes suspected could read her thoughts as well as having super-hearing, barked *Duh* in agreement.

THE CUTTINGS CLUB

St. Bride's Passage,
Fleet Street,
London EC4.
Tel. FLE 3232   27 March 2002

Dear Prime Minister,

   In accordance with your request we have pleasure in sending this latest batch of newspaper and magazine clippings directly to you instead of via 'the usual channels' (no names, no pack drill!) We have followed your instructions to highlight references to the Jubilee Cake and the government's handling of its preparation.

   Also as suggested we paid particular attention to anything that might have to do with national newspaper editors having been sent unsolicited foodstuffs through the post, but unfortunately (or perhaps not) we drew a complete blank.

   May we take this opportunity of wishing you a restful holiday weekend.

   Yours faithfully,

   The Cuttings Club

PORTIL-LOACH PROJECT SET TO LENS

Famed Brit director Ken Loach and obscure ex-politician Michael Portillo have teamed up in as-yet untitled project they plan to unveil at this year's Cannes Festival.

Story tells of young Asian girl from Midlands town (casting still in progress) who finds herself exploited after going to work in factory run by greedy socialist capitalist grandee (Saeed Jaffrey pencilled in). Forced to test pastry for **a celebration cake** she balloons out to 240lb and joins Weight Watchers where she meets and falls in love with equally house-sized but genuine salt-of-earth Ricky Tomlinson who appears in the buff in several unlikely but hilarious situations. Together they march on **10 Downing Street** to deliver a petition, losing weight and gathering support along the way.

"It's kind of Shrek meets Kes" says Loach, unrepentant about his rare foray into the commercial mainstream. "I want to give **this corrupt government** a good kick in the balls". Co-writer Mike Portillo is more emollient. "Hopefully this movie will show that far-left politics and caring Conservatism aren't so very different after all when it comes to highlighting people-exploitation. Not forgetting the Wizard of Oz feel with lots of big production numbers and Judy Garland type songs ".

The latter-day Don Quixote and faithful sidekick Sancho Panza met cute when Loach was on location with his last Spanish Civil War opus and Portillo was tramping the hillsides discovering his roots for BBC drama-doc 'Un Chien Andalou 2', aka 'The Andalusian Bitch'.

I am concerned about my friend the Minister for the Environment, Michael Meacher, and the frightful poser he has set himself: where oh where will he be spending his Easter break? The sad truth is, there just aren't enough days in the holiday weekend for him to do justice to his many properties!

Should he put those red boxes in the back seat of the ministerial limo and head south of the river to his Wimbledon mansion, or pack the green wellies ready for a quiet weekend at the half-million pound stone retreat in the Cotswolds? Or be true to his working-class roots, and nip up to his luxury constituency home in West Oldham? Or maybe a working weekend is on the agenda, calling in on one of his other six flats and houses dotted around the capital, and collecting the rent from smiling Meacher tenants?

One thing's for sure – there'll be no shortage of Agas, Raeburns and top-of-the-range microwaves to be pressed into service, that is if Meacher's boss **Tony Blair ever intends to get cracking with the famous Jubilee Cake!**

At the risk of sounding like my fellow tyke Fred Trueman, we didn't have **fancy Jubilee cakes** in my day. What we did have was an unshakeable self-belief and inner certainty that what we were doing was the right thing, hence there was no need to get the net out of the garden shed and go chasing after the dragon-fly of a fickle electorate in a desperate attempt to please everybody.

And we didn't spend our weekends worrying our heads (painted purple to keep nits at bay) about what would play best with the public. No, we sat down every Sunday dinner-time, regular as clockwork, to Yorkshire Pudding – the 'starter', as today's wine-bar Sidney and Beatrice Webbs would no doubt call it – followed by a boiled jack-rabbit caught in the trap that morning and two veg. from the allotment. Then for fun what we did was have a little jaunt out in the Morris to a lay-by on the A6, next to a notorious accident black-spot.

You see I don't need to go on the Des O' Connor TV show like the Prime Minister and make up stories about stowing away on an aeroplane as a kid. Hattersley has a very large hinterland, unlike the current crop of failed student agitators and dessicated city councillors who only politics know. And the current knickers-in-a-twist **cake impasse** (or chocolate log-jam, call it what you will) seems to me to sum up everything that's plain **wrong about New Labour**. They seem incapable of standing back and taking the long view. To them, success is merely the means to the end of further success, which explains why an unseemly panic sets in when everything doesn't go 'the project's way'.

So if you ask me if my main memory of 1959 is of a depressing third Tory victory in a row, I'd say no. It was the year of the blazing hot summer when feeling that I'd never had it so good meant getting my knees grazed blackberrying in the hills outside Bakewell. And tearing up my terribly indifferent school report into fragments of paper so my Aunt Augusta wouldn't get lost when she followed me home through the woods.

And floating downstream on the mighty Derwent River on a home-made raft with my best pal Tom Sawyer (later the Deputy Chairman of the Labour Party) hauling out catfish and clams and being cheeky to the skippers of the giant paddle-steamers that cruised by on their way up to Nottingham and Trent Bridge, where Larwood and Voce were whistling beamers past Don Bradman's ears.

That was my Old Labour. Dead in the water and loving it.

**The
Mirror** 26/03/02

JUBILEE CAKE WATCH
Only 68 days to go and still not a sausage!

PRESS COMPLAINTS COMMISSION

3 April 2002

Dear Tony,

Thank you for your letter. Unfortunately I can be of only limited help, since I stepped aside from the Chairmanship of the Press Complaints Commission over two months ago. I expect it escaped your notice, as the news was probably tucked away on page 24 of the newspapers as most PCC announcements generally are.

I sympathise with your problem. The death of the Queen Mother last month was I think it's fair to say a major national story, and it isn't terribly surprising that there should be (at the last count) over 14,300 websites putting forward different 'conspiracy theories' about how and why Her Majesty died, not one of which attributes the sad event to old age. The PCC of course has no control over what is purveyed via the Internet, though we have asked a gentleman called Jeeves if he would be prepared to join the ranks of our distinguished editors who sit in judgement on themselves.

Your argument as I understand it is with some editors from the wilder and woollier end of 'Fleet Street' who have alleged that the Queen Mother choked fatally on a piece of your government's Jubilee Cake. Headlines such as the Daily Mail's 'NOW BLAIR KILLS THE QUEEN MUM' are indeed regrettable and I will be pointing this out to the editor Paul Dacre during the interval at Covent Garden later tonight. This type of allegation can easily be dealt with by your famous Millbank Rebuttal Unit, but the other suggestion – that you have used your children as 'guinea-pigs' to try out the cake – is more problematic.

I can well understand your reluctance to either confirm or deny that cake has passed your children's lips, as such an admission could well be a hostage to fortune. My former colleague John Selwyn Gummer's career never really recovered from the so-called 'photo-opportunity' when his daughter Cordelia was obliged to eat a hamburger during the BSE crisis. The poor girl herself fled the country for America soon afterwards to escape ridicule, and I gather after several operations and changes of identity she has achieved some success under the name Nelly Furtado.

Clearly you have no interest in that fate befalling any members of your family, tight-knit as I know it is. But would I be right in thinking that your refusal to 'come clean' over whether or not they've eaten cake might have something to do with the existence – or not – of the cake itself? I ask because something not altogether dissimilar has happened to a friend of mine.

It seems my friend is involved with a very big international company which has been paying its directors and employees vast salaries, and keeping its stockholders happy, by pretending to make something when in fact it doesn't but just spends its time moving money around. Whenever suspicions arise – and this is where our friends from the press, though I love them dearly, can sometimes become a bit of a nuisance – what the company does is create or buy up more subsidiary companies and moves the money around that way…I'm not explaining this very well I know, and I'm not sure my friend understands it fully either, but what it seems to boil down to is that even though there's nothing there everyone carries on as though there is, and the company's accountants are helping to carry on this little fiction by destroying anything that proves there isn't (anything there).

Obviously I'm not saying that your government is guilty of such naughtiness, especially as I don't think your own 'company accountant' Gordon Brown would countenance such a policy for a moment! But I would urgently advocate that you do have something solid you can produce in evidence, in case these charges look to be in any danger of sticking.

I hope this advice is of some small service. My friend also presents his compliments and would remind you that his company has been a good and hospitable friend to your government in the past (remember the marquee with free bar and money at the last five party conferences?). So my friend hopes that this will be borne in mind in the unfortunate event of his having to go to gaol.

Best wishes to Cherie and the little ones,

Yours sincerely,

(Lord) John Wakeham.

CHAPTER NINE

'Events, Dear Boy'

I N THE SMALL HOURS of an early April morning Tony Blair gazed at his son Leo as he cradled the restless toddler in his arms. The Prime Minister's eyes were loving, but his mouth was set in the troubled expression that Blair found ever harder to leave behind when he stepped out of the front door of Number 10, Downing Street.

What kind of a world was he bringing the boy up into? brooded Blair. Where a seemingly innocent present from Silvio Berlusconi and the Italian people, would be routinely opened up at the Calais entrance to the Channel Tunnel and turn out to be full of asylum seekers, all complaining that the cake was too dry and short on fruit?

A world where his former Northern Ireland secretary Mo Mowlam would promote her autobiography on a camp late-night show on Channel 4, replacing her official bodyguards with half-naked Nubian slaves – and then accuse *him* of being on an ego-trip?

A world where he would be challenged by one of his own back-benchers in the House of Commons to outline his core beliefs? *Him*, the Prime Minister, having to complete the sentence "I like the Labour Party because..." in fifteen words?

Leo stirred and burped and a tiny bubble appeared between his little lips. Careful Tony, thought Blair with a rueful smile, don't you start frothing at the mouth as well. Beware of becoming Prime Minister Grumpy-

Trousers, like your predecessor John Major. Instead consider the lessons to be learnt from the unruffled demeanour of that other famous four-time parent, Her Majesty the Queen. Especially after what she's had to put up with lately.

Blair closed his eyes and, imagining himself in the role, surveyed the monarch's recent sea of troubles. Countless divorces and affairs. One daughter-in-law killed in a squalid car crash. Another hanging out with euro-trash and committing professional fergicide. A third in the royal doghouse after unilaterally arranging for Balmoral to be made over in an episode of the TV series 'Changing Rooms'. Teenage grandsons rounding out their Eton education at Spearmint Rhinos in Reading...and on top of all that the loss of both her mother and sister in a deadly each-way double.

How does she do it, thought Blair? Juggling the demands of a dysfunctional family and a busy career. Compared to that little lot running the government should be a positive doddle. He resolved to have an informal conversation with the Queen at the earliest opportunity, and maybe pick up some tips. The trouble was that his right-hand man Alastair Campbell and the Queen's equivalent Black Sod (as Campbell had taken to calling him) were barely on speaking terms, after the courtier with the ebony stick had pooh-poohed suggestions for rebranding the Golden Jubilee celebrations.

Campbell had commissioned 'Three Guys in Bow Ties', a cutting-edge public relations firm who had spent half a million pounds of new government money going through 1970s trivia manuals, before coming up with 'Highnessy 5-0'. But inexplicably the Palace had turned the new name down, even though Campbell had taken the precaution of first consulting HRH Prince Edward, who had enthusiastically given it his personal seal of approval in exchange for the TV-series and CD-of-the-theme-tune rights.

Behold the forces of conservatism operating full blast again, thought Blair, once more sinking into his personal slough of despond and frustration. What else could he do? Only that week BBC2's entire output had been a themed repeat of programmes from ten years earlier, which included scenes of the 1992 General Election. There recorded for grisly posterity were Neil Kinnock and Roy Hattersley, sashaying down the aisle at the notorious Sheffield Rally like Morecambe and Wise, to the strains of 'The Stripper'. Meanwhile a little counter at the bottom of the screen showed votes slipping away from Labour in their hundreds of thousands. Did people really want those days back again?

Leo was now asleep, and Tony Blair used the baby to prop up a copy of that month's GQ magazine. Hopefully it would supply some hints as to what colour combination of shirt and chinos he should wear, when inspecting crack British troops on his next sortie to a war zone. A familiar name leapt out of the glossy pages at him. Peter Mandelson had recently taken on the job of GQ columnist, a way of supplementing his meagre income from directorships and after-dinner speaking.

Idly Blair started reading Mandelson's latest offering. Then he stopped, disbelieving the words that were now dancing insolently before his eyes. He uttered a plaintive cry, undoing all the caring parenting work of the last half-hour as Leo immediately woke up.

"Et tu, Bobby??"

Conservative Central Office

Boris Johnson, MP,
Editor, The Spectator,
56, Doughty Street,
London, WC1N 2LL

4th April 2002

Dear Boris,

I have had drawn to my attention (by Alan Duncan, who is invaluable in sniffing out modern trends for us) an article by Peter Mandelson in something 'with-it' called GQ magazine. It seems he is behaving entirely according to type (homosexualist, I mean) and advocating in his fickle way that New Labour should do a complete u-turn and abandon their reliance on 'spin' altogether. Where 'black was once the new white', it seems that principled politics are now 'the new rock and roll'.

I need hardly spell out the catastrophic consequences for ourselves if this policy were to be put into practice. We have few enough sticks left already with which to beat the government and this would leave us almost totally bereft of effective sound-bites. The Dome has been a good friend to us, but I feel it is now subject to the law of diminishing returns, and in any case we haven't entirely ruled it out as a surprise venue for the cake we're preparing for Her Majesty's Golden Jubilee. Michael Heseltine has been persuaded to fetch his hard hat off the top of the wardrobe and go and investigate the possibilities for us.

I just had a depressing experience with some advisers I've had occasion to employ in the past, who made me sit down and watch a novel commercial that's currently running on the television. They told me that the Conservatives could do a lot worse than follow the 'soft-sell anti-advert' approach of Messrs Marmite – which would mean acknowledging that a majority of the population have thrown up at the thought of us for the last 100 years, so why change the formula now?

I'm sorry, but this seems to me to be taking Back to Basics a little too far. Mandelson as we know has the Prime Minister's ear (if that doesn't sound too homophobic, you have to be careful these days) so I'm seeking some advice from you Boris, as the editor of our party's answer to 'GQ'. There might be time to have a few words about the situation at the Queen Mother's funeral. I see from the seating plan that I've been put behind a pillar. Lady Thatcher of course would have produced a sledgehammer from her handbag and just knocked it out of the way, but I want to move on from that towards a more inclusive and understanding approach – someone has to sit behind it.

Onwards and upwards,

Iain (Duncan Smith)

PS I'm told your ladies in Henley are putting together some first-rate icing for the cake. Thank them on behalf of the party leader (me).

From the Secret Diary of
Andrew Motion, Poet Laureate

1.
On my regular matutinal pilgrimage to
A mall-becalmed Norwich bookshop
Intent (ignobly to be sure) on putting copies of a certain
Local Author's work in front of others no less
Worthy in the sight of God perhaps but paid considerably
   more
In hard cash terms during their term on Earth
I refer to Jeffrey Archer
Current resident of a local open prison
And as such apparently deserving of a prominent table
   display.

2.
But as I moved slim volumes of my verse to cover up
What Shall We Tell The President? and its noisome ilk
A shaft of dusty sunshine hit me in the eye, reflected off
   the
Embossed cover of another transient best-seller:
The Secret Diary of Adrian Mole.
I thought, we have the same initials he and I
And, like the flash that sometimes comes from ripping a
   plug
Untimely from its socket without first switching it off at
   the wall
The idea came to me: I'll do a Diary too

3.
So let this first entry be a private wail of woe
A Poet Laureate has only one pair of hands you know
First Princess Margaret had me biting on its nails
Now here comes the Queen Mum, fast upon the rails
And if that's not enough, he added bitterly,

It behoves me to produce another bugger for the Jubilee!
Helter-skelter come the calls and faxes, to-ing and fro-ing
With Downing Street's demand: how's the cake poem
   going?
The choice is stark, I sense: deliver something she can
   treasure,
Or else join Lord Archer at Her Majesty's Displeasure!

BBC

From: Nick Clarke, Presenter, The World At One – and voted Broadcaster of the Year, 1999 by the influential 'Voice of the Listener and Viewer'

To: Controller, Radio 4.

I don't have to do this, you know. Sometimes I think I'd be better employed carrying Alastair Cooke's golf clubs around for him than skippering your so-called flagship news programme, for all the gratitude I get.

Okay, so we won't win a Sony Award with this one. But before you read the transcript, bear this in mind. I was in there on a slow news day, on my own apart from some puffy actor who was more concerned about getting onto Dead Ringers than doing a proper job of investigative journalism.

So I see no need to apologise to anyone, any more than I felt I had to apologise to the people of Gillingham, Kent for confusing the place with Gillingham, Dorset (hard 'G') on the last Round Britain Quiz. They understood that shit happens, and so should you.

NC (aka 'A national treasure' – Radio Critic, Loaded magazine)

TRANSCRIPT OF 'THE WORLD AT ONE', 18/04/02

NICK CLARKE: It seems the Government's obsession with controlling national events knows no bounds and shows no sign of stopping, however inappropriate the occasion. How else are we to interpret the sheet of paper that was left in a photocopier this morning, just down the corridor from this very studio. It seemed to contain controversial suggestions for enhancing the Prime Minister's role in nothing less than the Queen Mother's funeral last week. Of course none of the radical proposals actually materialised on the day itself, so someone somewhere must have had a change of heart –

that is if the piece of paper is to be believed. We should of course point out that it is just a piece of paper, though that's what they said about Neville Chamberlain. And among the ideas put forward on it were:

ACTOR: 'That the Prime Minister should walk weeping and wearing a tall black hat at the head of a cortege of black-plumed horses from the East End that the Queen Mother loved so dearly, and in accordance with their noble tradition of ceremonial occasions, eg the funerals of Ron and Reg Kray...'

CLARKE: Once the procession had reached Westminster Hall and the Prime Minister had personally shaken hands and hugged each individual mourner, up to and including Her Majesty the Queen, he would then:

ACTOR: '...Lead the service, which would free up the Archbishop of Canterbury to mingle with the crowds lining the streets and cue the rounds of applause which would break out at regular intervals in response to the Prime Minister's eulogy being relayed Charles Spencer-style to the outside world...'

CLARKE: And the Prime Minister's role still wouldn't end there. Perhaps most bizarre of all was the plan for the burial service itself at St.George's Chapel in Windsor:

ACTOR: 'At the moment the Queen Mother's coffin is being lowered into the ground the Prime Minister will jump in after it and spreadeagle himself on top of the coffin, crying "You was a loverly lady! God bless you Mam!!"'

CLARKE: Naturally we contacted Downing Street to see if they had any comment but they declined to make anybody available. But this story refuses to go away, so to consider the wider implications we contacted the noted constitutional expert Lord St. John of Fawsley, who kindly broke off from mixing compost on the Prince of Wales's estate at Highgrove long enough to give us this statement:

ACTOR: 'This raises very important constitutional issues'.

CLARKE: Indeed. So what exactly were they? Once again we got in touch with every government department we could think of, only to be met with the same blanket refusal to comment. Finally we tracked down Jo Moore, the notorious special adviser to Transport Minister Stephen Byers who could be said to be one of the casualties, albeit at her own hand, of another recent royal funeral. This is what Jo Moore, on a bad line from South London I'm afraid, had to tell us:

MOORE: These are only rough outline plans and can by no means be considered government policy.

CLARKE: So far, so predictable. But after further questioning, Jo Moore went on to add this:

MOORE: Actually it sounds like a hoax to me – something to distract attention from the excellent relations the Prime Minister has with the Queen, as you'll see when they cut the cake together at the Jubilee celebrations.

CLARKE: So there will be a cake, will there?

MOORE: Sorry, my fridge is crapping out here so I've got to go and put some newspaper underneath it. 'Bye...

CLARKE: So, another piece of paper. Significant or not – what do you think? If you'd like to have your say about this or anything else you can contact us at the World at One website, bbc.co.uk/WATO – I should mention that Charlotte Green thanks everybody for their cough medicine recommendations and marriage proposals, and regrets she can't reply to every e-mail individually.

ACTOR: I can do her, too, you know.

CLARKE: Just time for the closing headlines...

BUCKINGHAM PALACE

From the Office of Gentleman Usher of the Black Rod

Lieutenant-General Sir Michael Willcocks KCB thanks Mr Alastair Campbell for his note of 18th April.

Sir Michael would like to assure Mr Campbell that he is in no way responsible for the 'leaking' to the media of the so-called 'Killer Memorandum', part of which was found in a photocopying machine at the offices of the British Broadcasting Corporation.

Not that it is any concern of Mr Campbell's, but Sir Michael does not even know how to work a photocopier. Any such duties that are performed in the Royal Household are the responsibility of the Lord Chamberlain's office, and specifically that of the Equerry Pursuant to the Xerox.

While appreciating the olive-branch nature of the gesture, Sir Michael regrets he must decline Mr Campbell's kind invitation to Burnley's crucial Nationwide League match against Coventry on Saturday. He quite understands that a place in the play-offs is at stake, but would point out that after a career in the services, most recently in Croatia, Sir Michael has had quite enough aggravation for one lifetime. Moreover, reference to *Who's Who* will confirm that his sporting and leisure interests are fishing, sailing and tennis.

Sir Michael does however wish the Clarets well against the Sky Blues.

TRANSCRIPT OF CABINET MEETING

24 April 2002

THE PRIME MINISTER: Sorry I'm late everybody, I was helping the Poet Laureate come up with a rhyme for 'cinnamon'.

THE DEPUTY PRIME MINISTER (RT. HON JOHN PRESCOTT): That's okay, we'd just about finished anyway.

THE PRIME MINISTER: Pardon?

PRESCOTT: Gordon, would you like to take us through the proposals for the Pudding?

THE PRIME MINISTER: Pudding? What Pudding?

THE CHANCELLOR OF THE EXCHEQUER (RT. HON GORDON BROWN): One, that the presentation be made to Her Majesty on the 3rd June, the first of the two Jubilee Bank Holidays. Two, that the Pudding be made earlier by volunteers from the trade union movement on a specially designated Day of Action...

THE PRIME MINISTER: You promised never to mention the 'DOA' words! I thought we had a Gentleman's Agreement!

THE CHANCELLOR OF THE EXCHEQUER: Three, that the Pudding will be divided up and given to the poorest members of the community, either in person or by post in an initiative designed to get the Royal Mail back its self-respect after the grotesque fiasco of Consignia...

THE PRIME MINISTER: Will someone call Security?

THE CHANCELLOR OF THE EXCHEQUER: Four, that the ceremony will take place at the Millennium Stadium in Cardiff. And five, that Her Majesty will not be given the unlucky South Dressing-Room.

PRESCOTT: Sounds good to me. Anybody got anything to add?

THE PRIME MINISTER: I'll say, how long have you got?

PRESCOTT: Not long. We've learned from your example, Tony.

THE PRIME MINISTER: Right. Okay. First, you know, will someone tell me – why a Pudding?

THE CHANCELLOR OF THE EXCHEQUER: It was thought that use of the term 'Jubilee Cake' or 'cake' in any context had become irredeemably associated with sleaze.

THE PRIME MINISTER: Ah, so you have been listening to focus groups! Point to me!

SECRETARY OF STATE FOR ENVIRONMENT, FOOD & RURAL AFFAIRS (RT. HON MARGARET BECKETT): No, listening to The Archers. It seems nobody wanted to be associated with anything endorsed by Brian Aldridge .

THE PRIME MINISTER: So what's the story with these trade unions? What's in it for them? They must want something in return.

SECRETARY OF STATE FOR TRADE AND INDUSTRY (RT. HON PATRICIA HEWITT): Apparently just a little recognition of their continuing importance to the Labour movement.

THE PRIME MINISTER: A likely story. I know those guys. They didn't come in on the last tram.

SECRETARY OF STATE FOR TRANSPORT (RT. HON STEPHEN BYERS): What's that supposed to mean? Guided transport is an integral part of future...

THE PRIME MINISTER: What's your take on all this, Steve?

PRESIDENT OF THE COUNCIL & LEADER OF THE HOUSE OF COMMONS (RT. HON ROBIN COOK): This should be good.

THE CHANCELLOR OF THE EXCHEQUER: Pay close attention, everybody. The trick is not to listen to the patter but watch what his hands are doing.

BYERS: Gordon's never liked me you know, Tony. Ever since

I was Education Secretary and I told those kids in that classroom that seven times eight equalled fifty-six.

THE CHANCELLOR OF THE EXCHEQUER: You told them fifty-four.

BYERS: That's what I said – fifty-five!

PRESCOTT: Anyway, Tony, everybody else is in broad agreement that a Cabinet Pudding is the right thing at this point in time...

THE PRIME MINISTER: A what?

SECRETARY OF STATE FOR EDUCATION AND SKILLS (RT. HON ESTELLE MORRIS): Cabinet Pudding. 'A steamed suet pudding containing dried fruit' – Oxford English Dictionary.

THE PRIME MINISTER: 'Steamed'??

SECRETARY OF STATE FOR HEALTH (RT. HON ALAN MIL-BURN): A little old-fashioned, sure, but very good for the digestion.

MINISTER WITHOUT PORTFOLIO AND PARTY CHAIR (RT.HON CHARLES CLARKE): And the skin, according to Peter Mandelson. He swears by it.

THE PRIME MINISTER: Well I seem to be outvoted, don't I.

SECRETARY OF STATE FOR THE HOME DEPARTMENT (RT. HON DAVID BLUNKETT): Hey, that's democracy – right, Clare?

SECRETARY OF STATE FOR INTERNATIONAL DEVELOP-MENT (RT. HON CLARE SHORT): 'Happiness, happiness, the greatest gift that I possess...'

SECRETARY OF STATE FOR DEFENCE (RT. HON GEOFF HOON): And the beauty of the venue is, we can close the roof of the stadium if it rains!

MINISTER FOR SPORT (RT.HON RICHARD CABORN): It's got a roof?

THE PRIME MINISTER: Couldn't I have just one 'Fruits of the Forest' special adviser?

SECRETARY OF STATE FOR FOREIGN AND COMMON-WEALTH AFFAIRS (RT.HON JACK STRAW): Don't tell me – Lord Birt.

THE PRIME MINISTER: He is a very experienced eater.

PRESCOTT: Sorry, Tony.

THE PRIME MINISTER: I think you mean 'Sorry Prime Minister...'

MINISTER FOR WORK (RT. HON NICK BROWN) Liniment!

EVERYBODY: What?

BROWN: Rhymes with 'cinnamon'. Sort of...

CHAPTER TEN

The Events Leading up to June 3

"Y OU'RE SURE YOU weren't followed?"

"Quite sure".

"Or that anyone else knows about this?"

Behind his steel-rimmed glasses, Stephen Byers first blinked in surprise, then narrowed his eyes in annoyance. Protecting his own back had become second nature to the Minister of Transport (or as the sign on his door now said, The Beleaguered Minister of Transport), and he resented the question.

"Absolutely nobody".

"Because we've been looking at your tapes Steve, and more often than not when you come out with something that definitive what you mean is the exact opposite".

"In that case you'll understand what I mean when I say quite frankly I'm very pleased to hear you say that, handsome".

"Gratuitous stroppiness that pisses off the audience. Love it".

"Do you?" Again Byers was taken by surprise. This was not what he was expecting from the interview. He took a thoughtful sip from his latte, in a mug which had a picture of Richard on one side and Judy on the other.

"They were less than nobody before they came here", said the bow-tied Bez, following Byers's look. "A fat frump and a complete half-wit. And now look. The Burton and Taylor de nos jours-ington. I'll give you another f'rinstance. Let's hear it for Mister Will Self.

Couldn't get arrested, even when he was coked up to the eyeballs. No one wanted to know. Consulted us - Shooting Stars, Today Programme – now he's on the short-list to take over the Jimmy Young Show. Mister Cuddly. Forget makeovers, Steve – we're in the Frankenstein business, baby!"

"And you think you could do something similar for me?"

"Working on it, Steve. Answer me this – were you boffing Jo Moore?"

Byers got to his feet. "This meeting is at an end".

Bez looked him up and down admiringly, like an art critic studying Tracey Emin's soiled bedclothes. "Groovy body language too. You really are the finished article, Stevo".

"I'm serious".

"Me too, deadly, so siddown", snapped Bez. "Do you want this gig or not?"

"Yes I do. And I mean that. Sincerely" said Byers, then remembered himself. "Erm, that is, no, I'm not in the least bit interested in the crappy job. Even the thought of it makes me want to vomit".

"Right – we're the good guys, remember? We're here to help. So wake up and smell the coffee-making facilities".

Byers didn't really understand this, but sat down nonetheless.

"Okay we'll skip the Jo Moore question. Just wanted a bit of goss really. Anyway, it creates an air of mystery, can't hurt. Let's look at your other qualifications."

Bez opened a file with a glossy cover photo of Byers in action, refusing to take responsibility as he inspected the wreckage at a recent train crash.

"Y'know Steve, you've got it all, man – the media's handed you a couple of diamond nicknames – "Liar Byers", "Pants-On-Fire" – yeah? You've consistently outscored Nasty Nick as the Man People Love To

Hate...and to cap everything you don't care about brazenly deceiving the House in front of the TV cameras".

"You mean...?"

"I mean, dude, that Celebrity Big Brother Two has just got its first inmate!"

Stephen Byers couldn't resist punching the air. His face was quite human and attractive when he smiled – which must never ever happen thought Bez, making a mental note. No sense killing the golden goose.

"Can I just let my partner know, before I resign from the government? Tell her to book that singles holiday?"

"Be my guest" said Bez, offering his mobile phone.

"I'll do it in private from a phone-box if that's okay" said Byers. "No witnesses, right?!".

He trotted out. Bez waited till the door had slid shut with a snake-like sibilance, which seemed to foretell what was to come. He pushed a button on the mobile.

"Bobby? Bez Trux".

"I know", hissed Peter Mandelson's smooth-as-dark-Swiss-chocolate voice. "You're on the display. One of my Favourites, dear. What news?"

"He's gone for it", said Bez. "Anyone else you want out of the way?"

BARCLAYS

The Party Treasurer
The Conservative Party,
32, Smith Square,
London, SW1P 3HH
24/05/02

Dear Sir or Madam, or My Lord or Ladyship

We regret we are obliged to return unpaid cheque no. 8368000 for £35.00 payable to The Latest Millennium Dome Company due to insufficient funds in your account, and your overdraft facility having been withdrawn after the recent party donations controversy. We have also debited your account with our standard £27.50 administration fee.

Please bring your account back into credit immediately, to ensure there are sufficient funds available for future transactions.

As part of our service to our long-established customers, please find enclosed the following brochures which might be of use in your present predicament:

MORTGAGE YOUR CENTRAL LONDON HQ AND RELEASE £££!

CONSOLIDATING DEBTS AND REDUCING STRESS AT ONLY 30% APR

NEW LOTTO'S CONTINUING COMMITMENT TO GOOD CAUSES

NEIL AND CHRISTINE HAMILTON'S BUMPER FUND-RAISING TIPS

UNCLAIMED PREMIUM BOND PRIZES 1979–2001

THE ANTIQUES ROADSHOW – DATES AND VENUES 2002

Yours sincerely,

Customer Assistance

MEMO

For: Cherie's Eyes Only

From Alastair Campbell

Date: 27/5/02

Subject: TB

All right, love?

I've tried everything I know, so could you try and buck his ideas up? It's just one public appearance for God's sake and after all it is the Queen's big day, not his. I mean, even Mikhail Gorbachev went on Russian telly once, advertising pizza to help raise money for a research foundation, how undignified was that?

The other point is that the wheels have finally come off the Tories' celebration plans, leaving the field completely open to us – I hear they couldn't even afford to pay the deposit to hire the Dome. If I didn't know better I'd suspect that one of the Blair Babes at the Treasury gave the Tories' bank manager a blow-job, if you'll pardon the expression!

Of course I know what's really behind the big sulk – it's because the whole palaver has turned into the Gordon Brown Show. Fine. No problem with that, personally – if I were the PM I'd just sit back, relax and wait for GB to self-destruct.

After all, the arrangements have been put into the horny – sorry, well-manicured – hands of the trade union movement. Pause for hysterical laughter at this end. Remember the News on Sunday? If they can't even produce a sixteen-page newspaper without blowing a pension fund what are they going to be like with a sixteen-ton pudding?

I'm sending over a copy of the programme for the day. As you'll see, there are any number of opportunities for the cameras to catch him laughing, crying, clapping – or pissing himself when the whole thing goes pear-shaped. If by some fluke it doesn't, there's always that good-natured cheesy face he maintained when Mo Mowlam got the forty-minute standing ovation during his Conference speech.

Did you see the picture of Steve Byers in TV Quick, drawing up a kitchen rota for the Big Brother House? That's my summer's viewing sorted out!

AC

BILL OF FARE

11.45am: THE BAND OF THE WELSH GUARDS
Elgar: 'Nimrod' from Enigma Variations
Vaughan Williams: English Folk Song Suite
John/Taupin: Jubilee Medley
(soloists: MR BRYN TERFEL &
DAME KIRI TE KANAWA)

12–3pm: Entertainment: MR BEN ELTON, CBE
('Nothing Too Saucy, Ma'am!')

3pm: Presentation of the Jubilee Cabinet
Pudding to Her Majesty by
Ms KERRY TE KANAWA (no relation)
(St.Hilda's College, Oxford)

3.30pm: Fly-Past by THE RED ARROWS

3.45pm: Entertainment: 'IT'S A WELSH KNOCK-
OUT' (Teams from Cardiff versus Swansea,
comperes MR STUART HALL & MR
JEREMY PAXMAN)

4.30pm: THE NATIONAL ANTHEM

CHAPTER ELEVEN

The 9.07 from Oxford to Cardiff via Swindon and Didcot Parkway

EXCITEDLY KERRY hurried over the footbridge to Platform 2 where the waiting train was being dirtied ready for her journey. Yet another platform alteration, the fourth since she'd arrived that morning at Oxford Station, bright-eyed and bushy-tailed (literally, she discovered, after one of her loony uni chums had joshingly tried to sabotage her brand-new outfit!) and looking forward to her big moment.

It seemed the gods were doing their best to conspire against her too. The specially-laid on flight from RAF Brize Norton had been cancelled, after a breakdown in the newly-privatised air-traffic control computer system meant that all incoming Heathrow flights were being forced to land on the M4. This was an uncanny echo of Tony Blair's advisor John Birt's plans for air travel, and more than justified his newly-created appointment as Unelected Uberminister of Transport. But it didn't make Kerry's journey any easier.

Nor did the ticketing policy in operation that day. Kerry had been forced to stand in a queue of customers who were angry to discover that using their Family Railcard to travel on a Bank Holiday meant having to leave their children behind. Finally she had reached the window and after using her Young Person's Timesaver to buy tickets for each leg of her journey (via Chiltern Railways, Great Western, Silverlink and Enronrail, formerly Connex West NorthEastern) Kerry arrived on the wrong platform with only seconds to spare and barely any time to look at her mobile.

But now she was safely on board, two men in different company trainers had blown whistles at each end of the 9.07 from Oxford, and Kerry's journey of a lifetime was underway. On her phone were text messages from the new men in her life. One was from her mentor Gordon Brown, wshng hr lck, the other was from her father, telling her a Viagra joke she'd heard ages ago.

The choice of young Kerry as a symbol of the meritocratic future to shake hands with the symbol of the oligarchic past (the Queen) had attracted widespread media attention, and flushed her father out of whatever Home Counties undergrowth he had disappeared into years before.

Oh well thought Kerry intellectually, it's closure of a sort. And her Mum seemed quite pleased to see the old creep again, especially after the disappointment of the Conservative Party cake. It didn't seem to have occurred to Joyce that she was making a habit of backing Tory losers. Her father had moved back in, sleeping on the sofa in the living-room, and luckily he had a liking for omelettes.

The train gathered speed. "Have you come far?" - that was a question the Queen was likely to ask, Kerry had been advised. She grinned. *Not 'arf,* she thought to herself, subconsciously doing the Alan 'Fluff' Freeman impersonation so popular among the undergraduates in her Oxford year.

Not far in miles perhaps, but an immeasurable distance cosmically since that day less than a year ago when she had been taking Pete for a walk and found the Cabinet papers on the canal towpath.

The train lurched sideways as it crossed a set of points. The top cup from a pyramid of empty polystyrene burger and milk-shake cartons toppled over on the table, narrowly missing splashing Kerry's dress with grey froth.

"That is sooo disgusting!" she shouted, then laughed at herself for falling back into the bad old helpless-victim Kerry ways.

No longer was she a member of the underclass. She was now a fully paid-up (or paid-for, to be pedantic) Master of the Universe. And anyone entrusted to hand over a ceremonial Big Spoon to Her Majesty prior to the Royal Insertion in the Pudding surely deserved to travel First-Class. It was no more than natural justice.

Swaying, Kerry made her way to the front of the train. This is more like it, she thought, surveying the rows of freshly-valeted empty seats.

"We are now approaching Didcot Parkway" came a voice over the PA system, only half-distinct amid the crackle of the guard's bag of crisps. "Please have your Enronrail tickets and railcards ready for inspection".

So what if I don't have a first-class ticket? thought Kerry Te Kanawa. I'll argue that my ticket entitles me to a clean and pleasant journey. And if that doesn't cut any ice, I'll pay the difference. I control my own destiny now.

That was the moment the train ran out of track.

Missing Track Theory about Local Girl Tragedy

A lack of track is thought to be one possible explanation for the derailment of the train from Oxford to Cardiff on Monday which killed local university student Kerry Te Kanawa as she travelled to the Millennium Stadium to meet the Queen. Among the many calls for a public inquiry into the crash is one from Dame Kiri Te Kanawa, who may be a distant relative of the victim.

By a cruel twist of fate Dame Kiri was due to be a guest soloist at the Golden Jubilee Pudding Celebrations, which were cancelled at the personal request of the Prime Minister as a mark of respect to Kerry (18), and it is quite possible that the two Te Kanawas might have been introduced.

The tragedy has left Berkhamsted traumatised. "She was the Golden Girl" said one resident of Shrublands Avenue where Kerry lived with her mother Joyce and father Gordon. "We called her Little Miss Sunshine", said another, a view echoed by local policemen Daryl Hall and John Oates (no relations). "Actually I was called PC Sunshine too, after a gang of armed robbers left me in a coma" added PC Oates "And for a while there Kerry and I got each other's mail by mistake, but that's Consignia for you".

Celebrity Big Brother

On the night after the crash and before official Railtrack investigators had time to arrive due to the weekend chaos on the M4, local residents say they heard workmen labouring through the hours of darkness to lay a new stretch of line, to make it look as if it had been there all the time.

An official spokesman for Enronrail, the company which runs that section of the railway, would only say "Apparently Ms Te Kanawa was travelling in first-class but was only in possession of a standard-class ticket, so she's only got herself to blame".

Enronrail was controversially awarded the contract to run the line six months ago by the then-Transport Secretary Stephen Byers. The *Gazette* tried to contact Mr Byers for comment, but he is currently incommunicado in the Celebrity Big Brother House. We will make another attempt after the first evictions have taken place next week.

The Connell Jackson Knowles
Literary Agency
(FORMERLY THE FRIDAY PEOPLE)

Joyce Te Kanawa,
278, Shrublands Avenue,
Berkhamsted, Herts.

6 June 2002

Dear Mrs Te Kanawa,

First let me say how sorry I was about the sad loss of your son.

But, 'always look on the bright side of life' as it says in the hit song, and we have a suggestion that might make the next few difficult weeks a little easier to bear. We're always looking for human interest and other light-hearted material that we can turn into books - just this week we've sold Jo Moore's Political Horoscopes for a tidy three-figure sum to a publisher for inclusion on their autumn humour list.

You may not know this, but one of the unexpected publishing successes of recent years was a fun tome supposedly written by Roy Hattersley's dog 'Buster' (actually it wasn't, and both Buster and Roy had a bit of help, little trade secret there!).

The word on the street is that while visiting your house this week to finalise plans for Kerry's funeral, both Tony and Cherie Blair took a bit of a shine to your dog Pete, and plan to ease your current emotional burden by taking it home to No. 10 Downing Street with them as a pet for the Blair kids, and something for Cherie to fuss over in the event of her feeling broody again. "It's the least we can do", someone heard Mrs Blair say as she stood cuddling Pete for the benefit of the cameras.

If this is indeed the case, we would urge you to let go of the dog by all means, but hang on to its artistic rights. That way we would be able to get a ghost-writer to come and sit with you for a couple of afternoons, get the lowdowns on Pete's likes and dislikes etc, and then weave it into the hilarious diary of what happens when he starts mingling with the movers and shakers of Westminster!

I'll try and call when it's not too distressing. Meanwhile hope the funeral goes well tomorrow (or today by the time you read this).

Love,

Pepsi Knowles

CHAPTER TWELVE

The People's Pudding

"IT IS NOT MY INTENTION to muscle in on private grief" said Tony Blair, looking into the middle distance over the sombre heads of the mourners on the quiet Hertfordshire hillside.

Gordon Brown closed his eyes. It had happened again.

The news of his protegee Kerry's demise had come through only minutes before the gas was due to be lit under the burners on the huge oven, out in the middle of the Millennium Stadium. The oven itself was a loan from a film company currently making 'Jack and the Beanstalk' at Pinewood Studios. The movie reunited the box-office smash 'Notting Hill' team of Hugh Grant and Julia Roberts (who was confident she could do justice to the part of the Beanstalk, though conceding it was 'a bit of a stretch') and starred former Arsenal captain Tony Adams as the Giant.

The oven deal had also reunited the team of Gordon Brown and Charlie Whelan, who used his media contacts to arrange the transaction on behalf of his former boss, promising the film company tax breaks in return for their co-operation. The Chancellor only discovered this later, but by then the project was history, and the pudding no more than ashes in his mouth.

"Kerry wasn't just a vampire slayer, she was *our* vampire slayer...She was the People's Warrior Princess" went on Blair. The Prime Minister was reading out selected extracts from the girl's Diary, and his voice rose tremulously as he gradually regained his confidence, dented after a week of being overshadowed by the royal festivities. He's relishing every treacly minute of this, thought Brown. Yet I came so close to pulling it off.

In truth nobody had quite believed he could. The Sun newspaper had even printed a large picture of a box of matches on its front page that morning, exhorting its readers to put their hands on it at 11 o'clock – the time designated for lighting the oven – and pray for a successful strike. "NOTE FOR SCOUSERS", the paper added, "THIS ISN'T A REAL BOX OF MATCHES, SO YOU CAN'T USE IT TO BURN YOUR HOUSE DOWN FOR THE INSURANCE MONEY".

> *"The tassel on the Oxford cap is stilled – it knows*
> *As clothing sometimes does, the ceremony is not to be*
> *Stained ballast plays mine host to crumpled sugar bags*
> *And twisted plastic stirrers; on such a bright June morn*
> *Both are pathetic, yet not, we know, a fallacy…"*

The words had been specially written by the Poet Laureate and set to music by Peter Mandelson, who had recently discovered that he was the great-great-grandson of the composer Felix Mendelsson. Dame Kiri Te Kanawa's voice soared into the sky, high enough it seemed to reach the jets that were 'stacking' above the M25.

This was more than Gordon Brown could bear. He reached for the remote control and muted the sound.

"Hey Jimmy, we were listening to that".

The other occupants of the Glasgow pub growled mutinously. Brown had come here that morning to be among his natural constituents. But they'd been drinking since 7am under the relaxed World Cup licensing hours, and recognised neither Brown nor the favour his government had done them.

Obstinately Brown changed the channel. The TV

above the bar now showed the build-up to the England/Argentina match later that morning – the funeral and the little 'do' at Kerry's house afterwards had been carefully orchestrated by Alastair Campbell to be over and done with before the start of the match.

The protests in the Scottish pub became deafening, booing and catcalls intermingled with a wolf-whistle or two each time Alan Hansen appeared on the screen. Several hands lunged at the Chancellor to try and wrench the remote from his grasp.

He switched to Channel 4, which was showing highlights of the previous night's Celebrity Big Brother. His old Cabinet colleague Stephen Byers was being berated by the unholy stew of soap opera bit-players, wannabe daytime TV presenters and stand-up comedians over accusations about whether or not he'd taken the free Rugrats toy from a box of cereal.

"Liar"

"Bastard"

"No, you're the bastard you liar"

"Piss off"

"No you piss off you lying bastard"

Byers seemed to be in his element, but the level of abuse was too much even for a tough Scottish pub. Brown was overpowered, the remote control taken from him and Kerry's funeral put back on the TV, which showed Tony Blair having to be restrained by his wife Cherie from jumping on top of the coffin as it was lowered into the earth.

Gordon Brown staggered out into Glasgow's Sauciehall Street. In the cold light of day he realised he had to go back, to confront his major problem – what to do about the mountainous raw pudding before it turned into his own personal Millennium Dome.

He stopped outside the Nessie Fish Bar, arrested by the window-display. A dozen Mars bars, deep fried in batter, were turning attractively on a spit, between the chickens and the doner kebab. The wheels in Brown's razor-sharp mind started turning along with these favourite Scottish delicacies.

Maybe he'd give the Granita restaurant in London a call. They were always looking for ways to freshen up their menu. Or, there was another possibility...

From The Desk Of The Delia Smith Corporation

Today's Delia Thought:

'Life is always Butter-Side Down!'

Dear Gordon,

Like the idea of the Pudding Slices in Batter. A tasty any-time snack, which would also fit handily into the plans for my new series 'Delia's Deep Freeze'!

Let's do lunch (as we say). I've got a window in February 2003.

Love,

Delia